THEOLOGY AND JOY

JÜRGEN MOLTMANN

Theology and Joy

with an extended introduction by
DAVID E. JENKINS

SCM PRESS LTD

'The First Liberated Men in Creation'
translated by Reinhard Ulrich from the German
Die Ersten Freigelassenen der Schöpfung
copyright © 1971 by Chr. Kaiser Verlag, München.

Translation copyright © by Harper & Row 1973

'The Liberation of "God"'
copyright © 1973 by David E. Jenkins

All rights reserved. No part of this publication may be reproduced, stored in a retrieval system, or transmitted, in any form or by any means, electronic, mechanical, photocopying, recording or otherwise, without the prior permission of the publisher, SCM Press Ltd.

334 01603 7

First British edition published 1973
by SCM Press Ltd
58 Bloomsbury Street London WC1B 3QX
Third impression 1982

Printed in Great Britain by
Richard Clay (The Chaucer Press) Ltd,
Bungay, Suffolk

Contents

	Preface by Jürgen Moltmann	vi
I	The Liberation of 'God' David E. Jenkins	1
II	The First Liberated Men in Creation Jürgen Moltmann	26
	1. *'How can I play in a strange land?'*	26
	2. *Domination through games and the preparatory games of liberation*	29
	3. *The theological play of the good will of God*	39
	4. *The human play of liberated mankind*	65
	5. *The liberating church – a testing ground of the kingdom of God*	76
	Notes	87

Preface

In his prize-winning essay *Uber den Ürsprung der Sprache* (1770), Herder called man the 'first liberated being in creation', after he had first described him as a greatly flawed stepchild of nature. Today we know a great deal more about the flaws of man and about his social and political misery than Herder did, but we are considerably less aware than he was of the joys of liberty and the pleasures of existence. The first thing liberated beings do is to enjoy their freedom and playfully test their newfound opportunities and powers. Why are we seeing so little of this? Have the old pharisees and the new zealots with their conservative and revolutionary legalism scared us away from freedom, from joy and spontaneity? It is unlikely that anything good or just will come about, unless it flows from an abundance of joy and the passion of love.

These sketches seek to reassert the value of aesthetic joy against the absolute claims of ethics. They are based on many conversations during my tenure at the University of Tübingen since the beginning of the student protest movement in 1967.

I dedicate these pages to my personal and literary partners in this discussion, particularly to the late A. van Ruler in the Netherlands, to Vítêzlav Gardavský in Czechoslovakia, and to Harvey Cox in the United States.

Christmas 1970   Jürgen Moltmann

I

DAVID E. JENKINS

The Liberation of 'God'

'Let God be God.' Such was the challenge and hope which Karl Barth, devotee and worthy disciple of Anselm, strove to present to the ailing Protestantism and smitten Christendom of the second quarter of our century. But, alas, refreshing and renewing as his great theological meditations were (and will be) to many, the pathology of Western civilization and the self-centredness of the Western churches and traditions strictly limited or blunted the liberating influence which Barth might have had. Further, Barth was, of course, himself a product of the European intellectual and Protestant tradition and as such had tendencies and emphases in his thinking which could easily reinforce, or directly contribute to, what I have already called the 'pathology' of the West and of the Western churches. Thus the actual effects of his theological work through many of those who claimed to draw their main inspiration from his was to reinforce those concepts of God as dominant and man as helpless which have proved so destructive. For it is they which have provided Nietzsche with his justification for seeing the liberation of man in the death of God and Freud with the pathological material which caused him to diagnose belief in God the Father as an illusion without a future. If the cry to 'let God be God' is to be truly an invitation to receive a liberating gift and not the infliction of a burden or a command to seek to impose such a burden on others, then we have to inquire very carefully into the understanding of 'God' which lies behind that cry or is likely to be aroused by it.

The extended essay of Professor Moltmann which forms the main substance of this book is, I believe, a most important investigation into the pathology of 'God' in the Western Protestant tradition, and it is as such that it starts many suggestive and exciting trains of thought about the liberation of man. At least, this would be my thesis about the significance of this essay, although I do not know that Professor Moltmann would understand it in this way. The essay is, in any case, tentative and exploratory, and it would not, I believe, be proper or appropriate to subject it to detailed and systematic criticism, even if I held myself competent to do so. Rather I wish to join in the exploration which the author exemplifies and to which he invites.

He says that 'these sketches seek to reassert the value of aesthetic joy against the absolute claims of ethics'.[1] What we actually see as the work proceeds is an impressive struggle to break out from under the burden which both philosophy and theology have imposed on Western man (and through him on many others) by being so much more concerned with the sin of man than with the glory of God. With this goes what has become a crippling failure to see the implications of the fact that this glory of God is expressed in a living (and as we might say 'truly human') man. (*Gloria dei vivens homo*, as Irenaeus first put it.) This struggle to break out of what has become a crippling theological heritage reaches its climax in the section in chapter 5 entitled 'The Augustinian Reversal', which is surely at the heart of the whole argument.[2]

In working his way all through this argument, Professor Moltmann shows a humility and boldness which are themselves an encouragement to join hopefully in the same struggle. He enables us to observe a theologian as he struggles to recognize and be freed from the present distortions of the theological rôle as he has received it. In so doing he is struggling to make his contribution to setting theology free for its proper task of helping men to realize the possibilities of their humanness in relation to God and the possibilities of God in relation to their humanness. This theological and human struggle of necessity involves an attempt to liberate men from the notions which they have had of God which have represented God as a man-denying tyrant, if not monster. Hence my title for this introductory essay, 'The Liberation of "God" '.

Here the inverted commas are an essential part of the meaning of the title. There is no suggestion that God himself needs liberating or could be liberated by the efforts of men. At least, no such suggestion is intended by me. Much recent and current theological writing does seem to continue to argue that we are somehow or other 'at the end of theism'. While it turns out that God, after all, is not dead, none the less he can be conceived of only as what might be called the immanently transcendental side of the whole evolutionary and historical process which finds its sole meaning and growing-edge in human beings and their becoming. Theological understandings of this type do seem inevitably to make the relationship between God and man equally inter-dependent in both directions. That is to say that they imply, or actually state, that God is as dependent on man for being God as man is dependent on God for being man. In such an understanding God's liberation and fulfilment is then mutually interdependent with the liberation and fulfilment of man. In this case there should be no inverted commas round 'God' in my title.

I, however, am quite unable to accept this position, however sensitively and skilfully stated. For instance, it seems neither to permit of, nor to do justice to, the sheer immediacy, dependence, abandonment and freedom both of worship and of love which sometimes comes upon us and which is witnessed to in so many traditions and testimonies of spirituality and exploration. Moreover, I do not think that 'the beyond in the midst' is sufficiently responded to, or represented, by focussing solely on that which is in process of emerging out of a past into a future. This 'beyond' requires also a recognition which is represented, or pointed to, by a vertical dimension going beyond into the depths and heights of what is, as well as a horizontal which is found only in becoming. There is a mystery and an Other which has its 'own place' as well as being encountered by us in our own places. Further, it just does not seem to me to be descriptively true in the world taken as a whole (e.g. in such a way that Africa and Asia are seen to be as important for human possibilities as are Europe and North America) that men are becoming incapable of God-talk or of concern for otherness, transcendence and mystery. Indeed, this is no longer as true as it was in the so-called 'secular' West.

It *is* true that traditional God-talk in a church context or from a church source is more often a barrier than a help, even to those 'within', and certainly to those without, in getting on to the transcendental and worshipful dimensions and possibilities in our lives. But this, I believe, is at least as much due to the pathology of Western churches and their theology to which I have already referred (but which I have not yet described) as to the secularization of our world-view and all the rest of it. This is why I hold Professor Moltmann's essay to be so important and suggestive. For I believe that by contributing to the liberation of our concepts of God and our ways of doing theology from the distortions which have entered into them, he is helping us towards a more healthy understanding and practice. These will make a most important contribution to our wrestling with the problem (about God-language, theism, transcendence, etc.) which has hitherto tended to be dealt with by various ways of asserting the end of theism or re-asserting traditional (Western) orthodoxy. If we recognize abuse, then we may perhaps prevent the abandonment or destruction of use, or learn new uses which do not lose the sense of pointing to the mystery, the otherness and the apophatic absoluteness which was contained in the (now admittedly abused) old uses of language about God.

Of course, the Christian faith and tradition does insist on and look for the most intimate connection and, indeed, union between man and God. This is the heart of the gospel and the fundamental significance of Jesus. Hence Christian theology and Christian devotion have the extremely delicate but glorious task of responding to the 'godness of God' and to the way in which he places himself at the disposal of men in Jesus and through the Spirit, which is quite as much an expression of his 'godness' (his very self) as is that which requires the language of mystery and of apophaticism to point to it. Hence God's expression of himself in his energy and activity for the liberation and salvation of men is so united with many human expressions of this same concern and hope, that the mutual dependence of God and men may seem the best way of describing God's commitment to the enterprise of being and becoming human as Jesus reveals this to us.

None the less, for reasons which I have just begun to indicate, it seems to me vital not to lose some grip on the notion that there is more to God (and not simply more to the concept 'God') than all that is involved in, and committed to, being and becoming human. Indeed I suspect that there is no chance of ever becoming fully human if being human is *all* that is involved in the totality of ultimate reality. For example, can we really contemplate with equanimity and realistic hope the notion that the face of God will turn out to be the mirror of the human countenances of 'me and all the rest of humankind' and *nothing more*? I do not believe that such a picture begins to do justice to the possibility and need of a 'Self' beyond ourselves in which we can and will find our true selves beyond all we have ever dreamed of and yet of which we sometimes get glimpses now. Moreover is it really truly human, truly personal and truly divine to think and to talk in terms of the world being fulfilled in *us*, however broadly 'us' is conceived? Surely, if there is a fulfilment to be looked for (or to be found and entered into), it must be a fulfilment of us and the universe *in him* who is either neither us and the universe or else both us and the universe *and* himself? All this quite apart from the questions of how a purely immanentist evolutionary optimism can be maintained in the face of today's threatened apocalypses or of what comfort and redemption it is now to particular persons and groups suffering in today's struggles to know that they are part of an evolutionary and loving process which will one day appear so.

If there is a God who really cares for the being, and becoming human, of human beings, it would seem he needs to be available directly and to be available now. This direct availability and presence of God, who *is* as well as will be, seems to be an essential part (and not just a mythological part) of the pattern of the biblical experience and of theistic experience (which is not, of course, confined to Christians). This has to go together with his absences, his incognitos and his presences, if at all, through representatives, but these latter aspects of the knowledge and presence of God do not supersede the former. His mystery combines both and goes beyond both. Thus it would seem to me to do more justice to the width of the range of experience which is behind theistic language and theistic pictures, to keep more possibilities open about the relationships between God and man, and to be more in accordance with the main thrust of the biblical and Christian reaching after God, to formulate the connection between man's hope of being man and God's way of being God in some other fashion than that which makes them simply mutually interdependent. It is not that God is as dependent upon man for being God as man is dependent on God for being man. It is rather, perhaps, that man cannot be man without God because God will not be God without man. The final and ultimate fact is God and dependence upon him. But this dependence embraces the unreserved commitment of God to man. (Is not this, perhaps, the mystery of the love of God for man? He does not love me because he needs me but because he loves me.)

I do not know that I am at all sure that I know what I am saying here or that I am succeeding in saying it. But I know what I am trying to do. I am trying to bear witness to a conviction which is growing upon me and in so doing to explicate this conviction even to myself. This is the conviction that the ultimate hope of fulfilment and freedom for man (and therefore for myself and for those I particularly love) lies in our total dependence. This is a total dependence upon God and upon everyone else and, indeed, upon everything that can be taken up out of the creative processes into the ultimate purposes of love. Dependence seems to me to be the one great hope of mankind and to be the only promise which has any promise of real fulfilment. Independence is not a reality now, nor is it a viable possibility for the future. It is an illusion that we can exist on our own and 'do our own thing'. It is, moreover, an illusion which if persisted in and acted upon can produce only destruction and not liberation.

But can there be a mode of dependence which sets us all free? For so much of the dependence that we now know is in fact part of a series of dominance/dependence relationships which we are discerning more and more to be humanly crippling, at the psychological, the social and the political levels. Thus the question of God is the question of the freedom of man posed in the form of a question about the possibility of a dependence which is, or can become, both total and totally liberating.

This, surely, also is what love is about if love represents or presents an ultimate reality which has a realistic power to be about anything. For love is an energy of relationships in which mutual dependence grows stronger than the unrelated or non-relating activities of independence in which and through which the lovers (who are also learners) threaten, rather than contribute to, the growth and freedom of one another. Growth and freedom go with the dependence and the dependability of maturing love. Of course, with us love, like dependence, often goes very wrong and we have many pathological expressions both of dependence and of love (they are often closely interconnected). So if we connect love, dependence and freedom, we are sharply faced with the question whether there are any sources and resources of redeeming and liberating dependence and love. It has been Christian faith and Christian tradition that this is precisely the concern and scope of the activity of God in Jesus Christ.

But how far does the record of the churches which claim to worship God through Jesus Christ support or encourage this claim or hope? This is where, in my view, we come back to the pathology of the West, of Western churches and of Western theology of which I have already spoken several times. 'Dependence' has tended to become a dirty word because dominance has been practised and exacted in so many ways which are now coming increasingly to be recognized as plainly dehumanizing (not that that necessarily enables us to do something liberating about them).

In the course of their history the churches have, inevitably, become permeated by the structures and practices of the societies of which they are part. The churches have, of course, contributed to their societies, but this process of contribution and interaction has, at all times, been symbiotic and two-way. A 'pure' church, in the sense of a body and institution which here on earth 'keeps itself unspotted from the world' and draws the hope of its existence and the direction of its actions only from God in Christ through the Spirit, does not exist and never has existed. It *could* not exist if it had to be part of, and play a part in, human society. For human society is a network of necessarily conditioned and necessarily conditioning interactions and relationships. Theologically speaking also, such a 'pure' church *should* not exist. For God did not withhold himself from the humanly conditioned condition of Jesus of Nazareth. Therefore those who are called to worship him through this Jesus cannot conceivably expect a 'heavenly' condition. If, then, the societally conditioned and necessarily human church is to be able to play any role as a 'people of God' and 'servant of Jesus Christ' it must be dependent on being always open to judgment and reform (cf. *'semper reformanda'*) by the Spirit. This involves being made aware, over and over again, of those points where conformity to, and being conditioned by, the environing society has reduced the church to false presentations of God, betrayal of Christ-like service and denials of and misidentifications of the activity of the Spirit.

We have, then, always to be on the look-out for signs of 'pathology' in Christian living, theological understanding and church institutions. We need to discern and deal with situations and conditions in which the living, the believing and their institutional expressions, have become sick and liable, therefore, to produce more sickness, rather than health and life. 'Sickness' here means a condition of morbidity which works against wholeness, growth and life. The so-called (and, often, sincerely believed) Christian actions are defensively self-centred rather than creatively outgoing, the 'Christian' believing is restrictive fantasy rather than expanding commitment, the institutional expressions promote submissiveness and fear rather than permit initiative and exploration. Men and women are thereby made 'smaller' in their living and their liveliness rather than given opportunities of enlargement into the infinite space and possibilities of the salvation of God.

Where pathological conditions and situations of this nature exist, or even become prevalent, then it is easy to see that the death of the 'God' who is obeyed in such demeaning ways, believed in in such restrictive forms, and represented by such dominating institutions, becomes a necessity for human liberation. The actual pathology of belief, of act and of institution produces the exact opposite of the 'salvation' which the believers in their actions and through their institutions claim to be both receiving and presenting. The way is thus wide open, not only for a Nietzschean proclamation of the death of God, but also for a Freudian analysis of the unhealthy illusion of the supreme projected Father-figure.

The importance, as I see it, of Moltmann's essay is that he is exposing much of the pathology in the Western Protestant tradition and expressing it as pathology. That is, he is pointing us to ways of seeing that neither this Western Christian tradition nor the nineteenth- and twentieth-century Western atheistic reactions to it are necessary expressions of and reactions to Christian faith and biblical understanding. Rather, we have to do with distortions and reactions to distortions. If we begin to understand this, then we may also begin to open up new and renewing prospects for Christian beliefs, actions and institutions which will be found, also, to be in continuity with fundamental insights and possibilities which have been overlaid by these distortions.

Professor Moltmann's way into offering us clues for detecting and dealing with these distortions is indicated by the remark in his preface which I have already quoted. (I say 'way into offering us *clues*' because, as he himself makes clear, his essay is a sketch and an exploration. It is for us to follow up the possibilities.) He writes, 'these sketches seek to reassert the value of aesthetic joy against the absolute claims of ethics'. I believe that a whole conceptual and cultural edifice which has by now outlived its human usefulness is challenged with overthrow by these mild words.

The edifice is that Western understanding of man which sees him as the doer of duty and the achiever of mastery, originally under a God who both dominated him and yet urged him to exercise domination himself. In its Marxist, and scientific and technological, forms, this view has discarded God, but the edifice arose as a Christian one. That is to say that it is the self-understanding of man which grew up and became the driving-force as European civilization developed and then pushed its influence around the world, while its commonly accepted way of understanding the world was some form of Christianity. It was God, the Father of Jesus Christ, who provided us with a mission which embraced the world and who was the source both of ultimate sanction and of ultimate reward. God was thus the Absolute who was reflected in the absolute of duty and responded to through it, just as it was God who was the author of the command and, as Creator, the provider of the tools to achieve mastery.

Whatever the appropriateness, ambiguity or distortedness of the original faith, insights and responses which were developed in the earlier stages of this European expansion, we are now living with its pathological aspects and effects. We have the ecological problems of the uncontrolled exploitation of resources, the political problems of white domination, originally of empires and now of trade and development, and we have the human problems of racism. We have also acute problems of faith. For the Christian churches and Christian believers have been very much part of the history which has, now, these pathological effects. 'God' is, therefore, very much involved. Consequently we are faced with the question whether what the word 'God' stands for is part of the pathology and nothing more, and therefore necessarily to be rejected as we seek healthier and more human states of affairs.

Hence the importance of this work of Professor Moltmann, which is a theological inquiry from within theology but under the pressure of political and other issues. The essay is a theological inquiry and reflection, written from a theologian's point of view and expressing a search for theological self-understanding. These reflections are based 'on many conversations . . . since the beginning of the student protest movement in 1967',[3] and throughout show an acute awareness of the human struggles of our time, especially for freedom or 'liberation'. But they are not directly about, nor, I suspect, directly applicable to, these struggles. They are re-thinking about theology and Christian faith in the light of these struggles and in their presence. This re-thinking causes Moltmann, as I believe, to diagnose pathological features in Western Protestant theology which are related to pathological features in Western society. I do not know that Professor Moltmann intended such a diagnosis nor that he would fully acquiesce in the interpretation I am putting upon what he has written. But I am arguing that he does in fact provide an example of the way in which the church needs the historical highlighting of sickness in society to be alerted to its own sickness and through this to discover what is available in its own resources to overcome them and thus be freed for the more effective service of God and man in the struggles of human society. In this case the human struggles for freedom occasion a re-examination of the ways in which the Christian faith has understood and represented the relationship of man to God. This re-examination enables a rediscovery and a reassertion of insights about God which promise to triumph over the pathology both in Christian believing and in society at large. The way in to the re-examination lies through an evaluation of the human importance of aesthetics and joy over against 'the absolute claims of ethics'.

In accordance with his approach as a theologian he develops this critique as part of his critique of theology as hitherto practised in his tradition.

> Theology does not have much use for aesthetic categories. Faith has lost its joy, since it has felt constrained to exorcize the law of the old world with a law of the new. Where everything must be useful and used, faith tends to regard its own freedom as good for nothing. It tries to make itself useful and in so doing often gambles away its freedom. Ethics is supposed to be everything.[4]

Now, to suppose ethics to be everything is to make a funda-

The Liberation of 'God'

mental and dangerous mistake about both God and man. Man is trapped in 'usefulness' and God becomes either an oppressor or an irrelevance. This line of understanding is expressed and developed all through the essay. A particularly clear summary of the main thrust of the argument is to be found in the passage commencing:

> In our society the training of children already involves such threatening questions of existence according to which the meaning of life allegedly lies in rendering service, being useful and having purposes. 'Be good for something or you are good for nothing', the beneficiaries of society are saying. When a man sees the meaning of life only in being useful and used, he necessarily gets caught in a crisis of living, when illness or sorrow makes everything including himself seem useless. The catechism question of the 'chief end' of man's life is already a temptation to confuse the enjoyment of God and our existence with goals and purposes. Anyone who lays hold of the joy which embraces the creator and his own existence, also gets ride of the dreadful question of existence: For what? He becomes immune to the prevailing ideologies that promise man meaning for life only to abuse him for their own purposes. He becomes immune also to a society which values and rewards men only in terms of their practical usefulness and their suitability as labour and consumers.
>
> It is not self-evident that we should glorify God and rejoice in him, if the world seems to us like a desert. The notion that enjoying God implies enjoying our own existence has been obscured by our Puritan training in self-control.[5]

That this is a *theological* distortion (which involves a false notion of dominion and domination) is well shown by the following:

> Karl Barth was the only theologian in the continental Protestant tradition who has dared to call God 'beautiful' . . . Another corresponding term is love, a love which does not merely manifest itself ethically in love to the neighbour but also aesthetically in festive play before God. [And surely, also, aesthetically towards the neighbour and the world? – D.E.J.]
>
> The one-sided emphasis on the dominion of God in the Western church, especially in Protestantism, has subjected

Christian existence to judicial and moral categories. Theology describes Christ as prophet, priest and king, but of doxology and the 'transfiguration of Christ', which is of central importance to the Eastern church, little has remained. The aesthetic categories of the new freedom have given way to the moral categories of the new law and the new obedience.[6]

The reference here to 'the Eastern church' is of particular importance, and all the more so if we follow up certain clues offered elsewhere in the essay. Moltmann writes:

> In the Old Testament tradition the term 'glory of God' is used in association with special theophanies and has a specific meaning. It describes an awareness both of the *fear of Yahweh* and the *glory of Yahweh*. Hence the *kabod* of Yahweh has pronounced mystic traits.[7]

This re-introduction into theological consideration of the notion of an awareness of God's glory in association with a recognition of a positive approach to 'mystical traits' is of great significance with regard to the liberation of 'God' from the limiting distortions of Western theology, in so far as its traditions have developed with a suspicion, and sometimes a hatred, of both mysticism and mystery. A God who is useful as the great purpose and upholder of the law and order of the universe in a 'Christianity not mysterious' can only become an oppressor whom it is a relief and a liberation to discover to be an irrelevance. (In this connection I should like to draw attention also to Professor Moltmann's comments on Marx's anthropology,[8] where he indicates that getting rid of 'God' does not necessarily get rid of the human subjection to the bondage of purpose and production.)

But a concern with the glory rather than the purpose of God points the way to many liberating possibilities. For example, the freedom with which theology has to do, and which is, indeed, the basis of theology, is well pointed to in the following:

> It is one thing to discover the *need* which makes talking of God necessary; the *freedom* to talk of God in that situation is quite another matter. This freedom is being offered by God alone. Theology therefore is both necessary and unnecessary. It has relevance for men in the realms of need and necessity. Yet it springs from man's wonder at the story of Christ and from his rejoicing in the uncaused grace of God of which it speaks. In

that wonder the realm of liberty is already entering the realm of need and necessity and bursting its chains. On first glance *Christian theology* is indeed the *theory of a practice* which alleviates human need: the theory of preaching, of ministries and services. But on second glance Christian theology is also an abundant rejoicing in God and the *free play* of thoughts, words, images and songs with the grace of God. In its one aspect it is the theory of a practice, in the other it is pure theory, i.e. a point of view which transforms the viewer into that which he views, hence *doxology*. The freedom to talk with God and of God is being opened by God's joy. It cannot be forced. For true awareness cannot be coercive; it does not come about by either authoritarian pressure or the force of logic. It presupposes liberty. Being aware of God is an art and – if the term may be permitted – a noble game.[9]

A 'pure theory, i.e. a point of view which transforms the viewer into that which he views, hence *doxology*' is surely a deliberate reference to the understanding which the theologians of the Orthodox tradition (and especially the Cappadocians) have of '*theōria*'. This is the spiritual capacity, developed by the grace of God received through fellowship and discipline of prayer, worship and a sustained pursuit of Christian discipleship in all things, to develop insight into the vision of God, both beyond all things and through all things. The basis of this capacity is understood as man's being created in the image of God and the fulfilment of the capacity, as of the image of God, lies in the ultimate transformation of man by the glory of God to sharing in this glory of God (cf. 'transforms the viewer into that which he views, hence *doxology*'). Hence we have one more piece of evidence of the way in which Moltmann is glimpsing resources for dealing with the pathology of Western theology in the traditions of the Eastern church wherein they have retained hold on insights and implications of the biblical faith which have become overlaid or lost in the West.

This is further demonstrated by the discussion of the glory of God leading to a consideration of the glorification of man which includes in its final stages the following:

> But what do we mean by the *glorification of man?* The First Epistle of John has pointed out that 'it does not yet appear

what we shall be, but we know that when he – namely God himself – shall appear, we shall be like him' (I John 3.2). Being a child of God by faith then means being equal with God. This does not imply an apotheosis of man, where man puts himself into God's place, but it does mean man's ultimate transformation to complete conformity with the visible God by seeing him face to face.[10]

This is a precise description of the Eastern understanding of man as destined for '*theopoiēsis*', i.e. to be made able to share the life of God. The Western tradition has always tended to fear that this means 'an apotheosis of man, where man puts himself into God's place'. But in its suspicion and misunderstanding of this doctrine the West has, on the whole, manifested its pathological tendency to defend the dominion of God by denigrating the possibilities of man, possibilities which are offered by God and stem from the very existence of God in his glory and love.

Thus we see Professor Moltmann redirecting our attention to the Christian tradition concerning the glory of God and man's enjoyment of that glory and in the light of that glory. This is a tradition which always had more emphasis in the Eastern church than in the West, but it comes now as antidote to those pathological developments in Western theology (as in Western society) which have magnified God by diminishing man. The end of this has been to encourage the dismissal of 'God' and a tendency to leave man enslaved to history and to production in a world which is suspected of being without purpose and therefore subjected to meaninglessness. Professor Moltmann is enquiring whether a liberation from a false theology of 'God' does not go hand in hand with the discovering of new possibilities and hopes about the freeing of man, and especially about freedom from the domination of ethics and purpose into the liberty of perception and joy.

Both his inquiry and, I hope, these exploratory comments and suggestions of my own can serve only to open up lines of investigation and, perhaps, to indicate that the issue of our understanding of 'God' is as important, and as potentially fruitful, as it ever was for our understanding of man. The wider implications which Professor Moltmann suggests as arising from his reassessment of the doctrine of God must be considered by the reading of his own essay. I wish, in this contribution of mine, to continue to concentrate on the strictly theological significance, and on the significance for theology, of the points which he raises and of the manner in which he raises them.

As I have suggested, one point of great importance is to be found in his convergence (perhaps both conscious and unconscious) with the Eastern traditions of Christianity. He is thus pointing us to a great reservoir of Christian experience and reflection which should and will prove of increasing importance in our attempts to face up to the present challenges of belief in and response to God. This also reminds us of the strict limitations of our own traditions and of the urgent necessity for the doing of theology with a truly ecumenical awareness. Perhaps before long the days of 'European-centredness' (or 'North-Atlantic-centredness') for so much of our theology will really break down, and we shall be liberated by the discovery that the future of Christianity does not depend on the future of our own version of 'Christendom'.

In connection with this 'parochialism' of theology, which has contributed so much to its pathology, I wish to draw attention to the way in which Moltmann summarizes the thrust of his reflections in the highly important section given the title 'The Augustinian reversal'. This section begins:

> After men have been *using* God for such a long time to enjoy the world, or at least to survive in it, God certainly does not promptly have to disappear from a world in which he is no longer needed for that purpose. If faith will only reflect on its true nature, we may come to a reversal of the things we enjoy and the things we use. Then man will *use the world to enjoy God*. The God who is a helper in need may disappear slowly but surely from the lives of many people and from our society as a whole. After the 'death' of this God we are going to be able to talk about the free God and how we can 'enjoy' him. When we cease using God as *helper in need*, *stop-gap* and *problem solver*, we are – according to Augustine – finally free for the *fruitio Dei et se invicem in Deo*, the joy of God and the enjoyment of each other in God. Purpose-free rejoicing in God may then take the place of the uses and abuses of God.[11]

For the full implications of this, it is necessary to read the whole section and to consider that section in the essay as a whole. The main drift of the argument would seem to be that theology, instead of starting from and concentrating on the duty of man and the sin of man before God, should start from the possibilities of the enjoyment of God. This is indeed a 'reversal' in Western theology (although not in Eastern). And Moltmann calls this an 'Augustinian' reversal. That is to say that he is asking for a reversal in the traditional order and focus of theology in the West to go back to that order and focus which Augustine held to be basic. (The glory of God and not the sin of man, not even the redemptive work of Christ to deal with the sin of man, is the most important thing and the starting-point.)

As we try to evaluate and follow up these sketches and suggestions of Moltmann I think it is worth taking into consideration that whereas he finds the clue to overcoming the pathology of Western theology in Augustine, there are those who see Augustine as a chief source of this pathology. This latter case is briefly and pungently put by Father Paul Verghese (of the Syrian Orthodox Church in Kerala) in his small book *The Freedom of Man*.[12]

He argues that Augustine's personal experiences and historical situation (his unsuccessful wrestlings with the acute weaknesses of his own will in the midst of the moral evil and decay of the crumbling Empire in the West) led him to produce a powerful but disastrous doctrine about the total sinfulness and helplessness of man. He thus over-dramatized and absolutized the Pauline insights about the struggle of 'the flesh against the Spirit' and 'laid the foundations for an idea deeply entrenched in Western culture – the idea that evil or sin is an integral part of human nature'.[13] *This* distortion, Verghese argues, leads to five 'basic distortions of Christian teaching (that) impinge upon us today'.

The first is a low view of the Incarnation. 'Regard the flesh, the body, matter, as evil, or even inferior, and one has already begun the deviation from Christian truth.'[14] I would further comment that it is this falsifying tendency to play down the material human Jesus in the so-called interests of his divinity that has had a large part to play in provoking the reaction against the divinity of Jesus in the believed interests of his humanity.

The second distortion of basic Christian teaching Verghese calls 'Flight from the World'.

As a consequence of his low view of the incarnation, Augustine undervalues this world. Or the converse might be the case. This comes out most clearly in the radical polarity he poses between Jerusalem, the city of God, and Babylon, the city of the earth. Babylon is the creation of sinful man in his love of the world.

Augustine's idea of the two cities comes up in the Western tradition in various ways – nature and supernature, nature and grace, world and church, law and gospel, the two kingdoms of Luther, reason and revelation, and so on. It is this basic dualism and the failure to regard the two as interpenetrating, that has caused much of today's secular reaction. Modern man refuses to accept a flight from the world of time into the unchanging immobility of a static heaven.[15]

Thirdly, we have the distortion of 'Man as Abject Dependent'. Augustine has too low a view of man. Verghese quotes passages where Augustine insists that man can do absolutely nothing good of himself and shows man as a beggar dependent on God. He then comments:

> This childish dependence of man on God is what Nietzsche caricatured as the slave morality. It is an affront to human dignity, and certainly not the view that Christ and the apostles hold about man. The 'world come of age' cannot brook this insult to mankind. It is not the Christian Gospel which undermines man in order to exalt God. It is too petty a God who can have glory only at the expense of the glory of man.

He adds:

> The assumption of polarity between the interests of God and those of man is perhaps responsible for the reactions of 'secular theology' and 'death of God' theology.[16]

The fourth distortion is described as 'Emphasis on Individual Salvation'. Augustine, in his soteriology, focusses 'too strongly on the individual man and his deliverance from personal sin'. This concentration on individual sin 'takes our eyes off the evil entrenched in society itself'. Further,

> By concentrating on salvation from sin, we are caught in a negative view of salvation. The 'image of God' view of salvation, as taught in the Eastern tradition, makes the demand that the

unlimited goodness of God has to be concretely manifested through the corporate righteousness of man on earth. Our secular theology moves away from individual and otherworldly holiness, to a corporate and this-worldly holiness.

Verghese adds the comment:

> Perhaps we are overdoing this denial of personal holiness and otherworldly sanctity. We need, however, to recover from a one-sided view of salvation as merely the deliverance of the individual from his sin. We need today a positive view of salvation which uses human freedom to discern and create new forms of social and personal good.[17]

Finally, we have the distortion of 'a low view of the sacraments'. On this, Verghese writes:

> Without the recovery of a richer sacramental view, we cannot recover a theology that takes the incarnation seriously. The world is good, the body is good. Without the body, there are no senses; without the senses, the human mind knows nothing. Christ has taken his body into heaven. Matter is the medium of the spirit. In fact, matter itself is spiritual – so the Eastern fathers would argue. If theology is to do justice to technology and culture, a higher view of the sacraments is necessary.[18]

Augustine is, perhaps, treated unfairly by being saddled with the full responsibility for these distortions. He is certainly unfairly treated if it is held that this is all that is remembered of him or to be found in his writings. There is much in these about the vision of God and about the liberating and fulfilling freedom of the dependence of grace which might enable Augustine himself to be the source of some of the antidotes against the distortions of 'Augustinianism' to which Father Paul Verghese points. But I believe that the five distortions listed do point fairly and squarely to the main sources of pathology in the Western tradition. Further, by tracing them back to Augustine, Verghese shows how deeply rooted these distortions are and how much work has to be done, with the help of all possible resources from outside the tradition, to liberate Western theology and its view of 'God' and, therefore, of man, for effective and joyful use in our present situations and struggles. The 'Augustinian reversal' of which Moltmann speaks will be neither effective nor possible unless the very different type of Augustinian reversal to which Father Paul is pointing is carried through. To work out what it means today to find the central motif of theology and the central motivation of Christian individual and corporate action in, first, the glory of God and, then, man as in the image of God, destined to share that glory and already showing signs of it, will be an immense task. But it is surely also an immensely promising and rewarding one. It will be a getting back to authentic Christian insights by going on to pressing human tasks and exciting human possibilities.

Here I wish to turn, by way of a final introductory comment and exploratory query, to the political and social side of Moltmann's essay. He begins by rightly asking how we can speak of joy at such a time as this, and he continues to insert apposite reminders about the agonies and uncertainties of our times and of the inhuman dealings of man with man. A good example of this is his recalling of Bonhoeffer's reproach 'We have no right to chant in the Gregorian mode, if we fail to cry out for the Jews.'[19] We certainly have no right to talk of joy in the glory of God and freedom through dependence upon God if we use this talk to turn away from the political struggles, the economic sufferings and the human frustrations of our time. It would be no liberation of the concept of 'God' to turn from a degrading dominance fantasy to a regressive escapist one.

We need, therefore, to take into very serious consideration the references which Moltmann makes throughout his discussion to the cross of Jesus (including his remark 'I think we should literally and sincerely leave the cross out of the game').[20] The way in which he attempts to bring together both joy and political concern is well indicated, for example, in his discussion of repentance which includes the following:

> The *vision of God* comes to life by following the crucified with permanent *repentance* and through constant *changing* of existing conditions. It cannot be obtained apart from this . . . Transfiguration cannot be demonstrated on a mountain away from the world. Even the transfiguration of Jesus took place on the road to Jerusalem and the cross. The transfiguration of the unveiled face must be demonstrated in a suffering and struggling transformation which involves changing oneself and existing

conditions so that man, together with other men, may be conformed to his future . . .

Man is not liberated from his old nature by imperatives to be new and to change, but he rejoices in the new which makes him free and lifts him beyond himself. Where repentance is understood as a spiritual return to the evil and rejected past, it deals in self-accusation, contrition, sackcloth and ashes. But when repentance is a return to the future, it becomes concrete in rejoicing, in new self-confidence and in love . . . [The Occidental tradition of repentance] has been unable to demonstrate either practically or theoretically the gospel of the joy of God and the liberation of man. But if repentance as return to the future already is rejoicing in freedom, then out of that joy it should also be possible to bring about changes of unjust and oppressive social and political conditions.[21]

But despite discussions of this nature and powerful and provocative suggestions such as those contained, for example, in the sections 'The Augustinian reversal' and the one following, entitled 'Experiments in the realm of freedom', I cannot escape the suspicion that Professor Moltmann has not yet found the theological way, nor all the theological clues necessary for the way along which we can understand and respond to the dynamic and creative relations between the glory of God, the glory and joy of man and the struggles and sufferings of man. This is not to be wondered at, nor is it a negative criticism of his attempt so far, for the task is an exceedingly difficult one and requires trial essays of the type which we are offered here and which will have to combine exploration with incompleteness.

The difficulty lies in the possibility that the sudden interest in 'play' (which is to be found arising on both sides of the Atlantic) is largely (and too much) conditioned by the emergence of the space and need for a 'leisure culture' in the too-affluent and so-called incipiently 'post-industrial' societies. This may go together with a felt need to turn away from the threatening demands for radical and revolutionary change which arise if the condition of the affluent countries is seriously considered in the light of the conditions in the Third World and of the conditions of many poor and underprivileged within the affluent countries themselves. Talk of 'play' could therefore be a bourgeois device to protect the enjoyment of the bourgeoisie. Further, theologians might take up this talk both because we are of the bourgeoisie and because it is in fashion. Thus we should find a way of making a case for theology and, indeed, continue to attempt to operate theology as a normative, or at least a justifying, activity. (Play-talk is good and profitable talk because it is God-talk.) This would, of course, mean that we were not concerned with the liberation of 'God' but were passing from bondage to bondage, though choosing a new form of bondage which might allow us, also, to retain some form of domination and influence.

The matter is a very difficult and delicate one, and the disturbing questioning involved cannot be properly faced if it is simply addressed at Professor Moltmann. It must be addressed to oneself. Here it seems to me necessary to admit that the escapist element in theologizing and in the account that one gives to oneself of what is involved in faith is always present and always liable to promote self-protecting distortions. Moreover, Christians corporately, either as loosely organized groups or through their ecclesiastical institutions, are always in danger of giving expression to these same distortions. Thus 'fashions' in theology may be only a defensive and self-centred response of some sections of the church to threatening features in contemporary developments, rather than a rediscovery and renewal of realistic and powerfully effective elements of the authentic tradition and faith.

I believe that the rediscovery and reapplication of insights about glory, joy and play will prove authentic and effective only as we struggle to discover what it now means for us that the glory of God, which is the destiny of man, was embodied in the crucified man, Jesus, who, in himself, is God. But to explore this I think that we shall have to dissent from Moltmann's recommendation that 'we should literally and sincerely leave the cross out of the game'.[22] This remark, although understandable in its context, seems to me to indicate that the pathologies, or at least the distorting limitations, of Western theology which were to be overcome by the so-called 'Augustinian reversal', are still in danger of exerting their influence.

In one of his criticisms of Augustine and the Western tradition which I have already cited,[23] Father Paul Verghese calls attention to 'this basic dualism and failure to regard the two as interpenetrating'. He is referring to potentially dualistic pairs like 'nature and supernature, nature and grace, world and church, law and gospel, the two kingdoms of Luther, reason and revelation, and so on'. The crucial notion here for our purposes is, I believe, that of *interpenetration*. There is something which the West has not seemed able to contemplate or work with. Until comparatively recently, Western theological thought has been able to tolerate and even deal in metaphysical, theoretical and formal mysteries wherein entities conceived of as substances or forces which are by definition distinct none the less interact in ways which are supposed to preserve their separate identities intact. Even when the modes of thinking were acceptable, the practical effect tended to be that one side of the pair obliterated the other. Thus the divine dominated, disturbed, diminished the human. This tendency, together with the breakdown of the appropriate modes of thinking in any case, resulted in the reassertion of the human to the exclusion of the divine.

However, the notion of 'interpenetration' belongs to an approach which thinks and feels in terms of an energetic dynamic and organic intermingling which is working, struggling and flowing both from and to a mystery of union. We have to do, not with an interaction of separateness, but with an interpenetration of potential mutuality.

What I am afraid of, is that Professor Moltmann has simply 'reversed', but not basically changed, the Western dualistic way of thinking. Thus, he wishes, rightly, to overcome the effects of concentration on the sin of man, on the usefulness of God's redemption in saving man from sin, and on the consequent duties and opportunities open to man in working out his salvation in developing and dominating the world and society. He wishes to question the primacy of ethics and reopen the possibilities and freedoms of joy. He wishes also to relate those new (or renewed) insights about joy and freedom to the human need of, and struggles for, changed conditions and a changed society. But his working out of his approach (at least as far as it goes in the essay which follows) leaves me with the feeling that he is in danger of 'reversing' the debilitating and demeaning effect of theological concentration on sin, redemption and duty by producing a focussing on the glory of God and the joy and enjoyment of man which is somehow 'outside' the human oppression, struggles and need for change. He clearly intends his discussion to be relevant *to* these struggles, but it is difficult to see or feel how the glory and the joy are involved *in* them. There is a lack of interpenetration. Hence the way is open for the suspicions which I have raised about theological talk about play being a device to deflect attention from the real seriousness of the needs and demands of society for radical change.

It is here, therefore, that I see the need to question the remark about advising us to 'leave the cross out of the game'. Moreover, I would suggest that a deeper exploration into the insights of the Eastern tradition, including their understanding of the interpenetrations of the divine and the human, would enable us to understand that, on the one hand, the cross can never be 'left out of the game', but that, on the other, we are always concerned with a joyous struggle that has to do with glory. Jesus Christ, who is the man who is God and God become man, is the reality who represents to us that struggle and joy, suffering and transcendent calm, interpenetrate in the life of God and in human life, as we seek the fulfilment of our being and becoming in the image of God.

I had better say at once that I have nothing concrete to say here about what that would mean in practice. All I could do has been to point to some directions of exploration which seem to be opened up, or reopened up, by Professor Moltmann's essay. I have also tried tentatively to suggest one point where these explorations might be guided with the help of closer attention to the resources and insights of the Eastern Orthodox tradition and experience. I believe that these explorations put us on the track of three developments which are central to the liveliness of Christian faith and the practice of human hope.

The first is a liberation of 'God', the second is the increasing discovery of a dependence which is a mutuality, an interpenetration and a sharing, and the third is the development of a radical spirituality combined with a radical concern for politics. The three are in fact closely interconnected. It is both necessary and promising to free 'God' from the connotations of dominating dependency and a demand for an obedience which diminishes men. For it is thus that the idea of 'God' and the worship of God and the attempts at obedience to God have become corrupted, especially in the Western tradition. Thus both the transcendence and the availability of God, his presence and his distance, his energies and his space for human response and initiative, can become newly available to men as the beyond in the midst and the beyond who is a still-centre and an unshakeable certainty over and above all that we know or do or cannot know and fail to do. In this knowledge and experience will be the possibility and beginnings of a dependence which sets one free for openness to everything and for the change and renewal of all that hampers, hinders, frustrates and encloses. In so far as we grow in the knowledge and practice of dependence upon an infinite love whose energy is constantly at work to create and evoke an equally energetic, authentic and self-expressive response, we shall discover the strength, the insight and the motivation to exercise our independence of every passing problem, temporary institution, or accepted purpose and demand which in fact turns out to be something restrictive, distorting or frustrating of wider human mutuality and development. Without the certainty and encouragement of a dependence which is both total and totally creative, it will not be possible to have the courageous identity which must fight against everything, however well supported or honoured by time, custom, science or public opinion, which shuts men and women up in lesser things than their divinely human destiny.

Hence the liberation of 'God' and the discovery of the possibilities of a creative and liberating dependence should enable us to enter into that radicality of politics which will set us at effective criticism of all the social structures and practices which men use to deprive other men of equal opportunities for humanness. We shall be so set free because we shall also be entering upon a radical spirituality which is moving us always closer to the reality of the infinite God who committed his energies to becoming a crucified man and continues this energy as an offer to emerging human beings as the very Spirit who is himself. The sufficiency for this radicality will therefore be found to be of God. But it will be found to be an offer to us as we seek to be men and women who are at the disposal of, and ready to lose ourselves in, the struggle to enable the humanness of men and women in the midst of all of today's conflicts, sufferings and possibilities. What we seek, and what we are offered, is the interpenetration of the infinity of God with the frailties, frustrations and joys of present human beings, together with the promise of a future which is, at the same time, divine and human because the one is to be fulfilled in the other. This is the way joy lies, and it is a possible and proper joy because it includes the cross and because the cross is at the historical heart of the enabling and liberating of this joy.

I believe it is such vistas and such practices which Professor Moltmann's essay helps to point us to and start us on. But it must always be remembered that actual play, actual joy and the actual doing of concrete politics can never be written about – or certainly not written about in advance. They might be celebrated after the event, if we had the poetry for it. Therefore the most that can be expected of theological reflection of this sort is that it should clear the ground and, perhaps, in so doing point also to possibilities which can be taken up in the exploration of living. The true witness to God, and the true expression of the real possibilities both of joy and of glory, will be found among those who can sing in exile, rejoice in struggle and glimpse glory in hope as yet frustrated, because they have discovered, usually through one another, that the infinite distance of God is the measure of the power of his presence and that the suffering of God is the measure of the power of his untroubled and invincible love.

Easter 1973

II

JÜRGEN MOLTMANN
The First Liberated Men in Creation

1. 'How can I play in a strange land?'

Every man has a burning desire for happiness and enjoyment. But our world gives us little cause for rejoicing. To be happy, to enjoy ourselves, we must above all be free. But such freedom has grown scarce. We enjoy ourselves, we laugh, when our burdens are removed, when fetters are falling, pressures yield and obstructions give way. Then our hearts leap within us and we suddenly find it easy to cope with other men and circumstances. We gain distance from ourselves and our plans move forward in a natural, unforced way. There is also, of course, a kind of laughter which bursts out in despair, we can laugh at others with scorn, and there is the snobbish smile or the cynical grin. But jubilant, liberating laughter is always unburdening and burdenfree. But how can we laugh, how can we rejoice without care, when we are worried, depressed and tortured by the state of the world in which we live? It sounds good to hear the promise of Psalm 126: 'When the Lord restored the fortunes of Zion, we were like those who dream. Then our mouth was filled with laughter. . . .' But we do not yet find ourselves in that condition. In our situation we would rather ask with Psalm 137: 'How shall we sing the Lord's song in a foreign land?' or complain with an old black spiritual from slave days: 'How can I play, when I'm in a strange land?'

How can we laugh and enjoy ourselves when innocent people are being killed in Vietnam? How can we play when children are starving in India? How can we dance when human beings are being tortured in Brazil?

Are we not living in *one* world? Is it right to laugh, to play and to dance without at the same time crying out and working for those who perish on the shadowy side of life? Does it not seem that the cultural revival of play, festivities and enjoyment in the affluent West is forced and downright unnatural as long as there are such hells on earth? *Homo ludens* and the redemption of our right to happiness, fun and games appear to be fine – but only for those who can afford them. To all others they must appear in bad taste.

When in spite of all this I dare to talk about the enjoyment of our freedom and our pleasure in play, I am not addressing myself to those who are incapable of feeling, of mourning and suffering with others because they are deceiving themselves with their shallow, self-satisfied optimism. I am turning to those who are mourning and suffering with others, who are protesting and feeling oppressed by the excess of evil in their society, who are weighed down by their own impotence so that they are either ready to despair or seek to forget.

How can I play in a strange land, in an alienated and alienating society? How can we laugh and rejoice when there are still so many tears to be wiped away and when new tears are being added every day?

Some time ago the play *Anatevka* or *Fiddler on the Roof* made the circuit of our stages. It tells of Tevye, the dairyman, and his Jewish congregation in the Ukranian village of Anatevka. The Czar is oppressing them with excessive taxation. Their sons have to serve in a strange army and fight in unwanted wars. The Cossacks initiate pogroms against them whenever it strikes their fancy to go after the Jews. Still, this small congregation of the persecuted and pursued is singing the Lord's song in an alien land. Are they doing this merely to forget their ugly predicament? Are they only trying to comfort themselves by covering their sadness with happy sounds? Or is there really such a thing as freedom in the midst of slavery, joy in the midst of suffering, and praising God in the groaning of his creatures?

If we are to gain an understanding of this mystery, we will have to inquire critically what constitutes laughter in its tortured and liberated forms. What are the patterns and functions of fortune, play and enjoyment in our society? We must learn to distinguish between the alienated forms of merely apparent good fortune and the liberating forms of enjoyment. Conversation, diversion and amusement can easily cheat us out of the dangerous but genuine good fortune of freedom. Yet, on the other hand, it is possible that in playing we can anticipate our liberation and with laughing rid ourselves of the bonds which alienate us from real life.

2. Domination through games and the preparatory games of liberation

Critical game theory

Since the French Revolution and the dawn of the industrial age numerous cultural and political theories have been proposed which seek to understand the meaning and significance of play in human life. But hardly any of these are based on the existing social realities and political functions of playing.[1] Play has become a theoretical problem only since man has been forced into disciplined, rationalized labour in constantly growing industrial complexes and since playfulness has been banned from the realm of labour as mere foolishness. The discussions about the nature of games, therefore, have overtones of a romantic or utopian longing for a simple childhood world which has either been lost or not yet been reached. In an age of industry and machines we tend to associate our fondness for play with a melancholy criticism of our modern culture and its alleged loss of childlike innocence, of ancient good and religious values. The average European – conditioned as he is to self-control and reflection – experiences in an altogether primal fashion his own pitiful awkwardness when he happens to observe people in Africa or in Latin America singing and dancing, people he otherwise tends to denigrate as 'primitives' or 'natives'.

Yet the industrial revolution, which has deprived its participants of their games, is merely a concomitant of the political rebellions which had their origins in the French Revolution. If we examine the early theories about play in Germany, we find that they were stimulated precisely by that revolution and were intended intellectually and culturally to neutralize it. Friedrich Schiller, who at first had been an enthusiastic supporter, turned his back on the French Revolution following the September murders instigated by Marat. His work, *Über die ästhetische Erziehung des Menschen*,[2] is still today the point of departure for many investigations of the problem of play. For him aesthetics takes the place of political liberation. 'The path to freedom leads through beauty,' he says in his *Second Letter*. For 'where everything is rotten, only the most beautiful of the arts is free from political rot'. In the beautiful illusion of the arts the revolution of liberty finds its completion after it has been strangled in political abuse and misfortune. 'Here, then, in the realm of aesthetic illusion, we have reached the ideal of equality which so many enthusiasts would like to see realized in its essence as well.' So a *true republic*, like a *true church*, exists only within the select circles of beautiful souls.

> Flee to the quiet chambers of the heart
> Depart the pressing turmoil of men's lives.
> Freedom reigns but in the land of dreams,
> Beauty blossoms only in a song,

wrote Schiller and many German intellectuals agreed with him, since they had lived through the French Revolution in mind only and were willing to accept it merely as a 'revolution of the mode of thinking'.

Those who would have liked to see the happy state of 'liberty, equality and fraternity' realized politically were dubbed *enthusiasts* (*Schwärmer*), when in truth the real 'enthusiasts' are those who 'enthuse' about freedom only aesthetically and at the same time make their peace with political bondage and legal inequality. A purely aesthetic interest in the liberty of game playing is not counter-revolutionary, as some of the hard-bitten revolutionary realists contend. Rather it constitutes a well-known and constantly observable transformation of a messianic hope for change into a mysticism of a better world, the metamorphosis of an outward disappointment into an inward emigration and of a political defeat into a journey of discovery for the soul. The enthusiasts of the Reformation period moved from mysticism to political revolt, and after that failed, became quietists. Many of the neo-mystics and hippies in America hail from the frustrations of the civil rights movement. So the freedom of playing becomes a substitute for political liberties which could not be achieved. But the political aspirations in turn are preserved in those very game patterns of the 'inner light' in anticipation of more favourable circumstances.

All the theories about play make the point that a game is meaningful within itself but that it must appear useless and purposeful from an outside point of view. Just asking for the purpose of a game makes a person a spoilsport. Game theories therefore never raise the question of the *Sitz im Leben*, of the place playing occupies in contemporary society, and they tend to overlook the social and political functions of contemporary games. As a result the topic becomes redundant, since it has been divorced from the natural context of interest into which game playing factually belongs. The topic 'play' is in itself misleading, since play is regarded as a means of escape from the rest of the world. Theory merely looks at the play itself and thus becomes accessible to any kind of interest.

A *critical theory of play* must begin with the question: *Cui bono? Whom does it serve?* Of course, this may sound like the miserable mood of a spoilsport, but the question really serves only to unmask those who cheat at the game. Given a society where man's labour alienates and empties him, where of necessity even the games of recreation and leisure, the arts and social functions bear the marks of estrangement from real life, it is clearly impossible to describe a real and wholesome life simply in terms of the aesthetic categories of that very same society. Assurances to the contrary notwithstanding, such attempts consistently leave the impression of being merely playful and snobbish, an impression we can ill afford as long as our society remains as it is now and tends to deform man, as we have indicated, which in fact it frequently does. We intend therefore to concern ourselves critically with the games of today starting with a critical analysis from the outside. This does admittedly constitute an approach foreign to an understanding of the game as self-forgetting pleasure. But it may be that our eyes are opened to the truly familiar only as we become alienated from what is alienating. We shall attempt to move from a critical analysis of games in terms of their outward appearance in society to a critical analysis of society in terms of an inside view of games. At first a person may refuse to keep on playing because he has become suspicious of the sponsors of the game. Later he decides to play anyway because he wants to put the sponsors out of business. Then he is no longer playing for them but against them.

Bread and games

Panem et circenses was the motto of the Roman imperial rulers: Let us give bread to the people and they will be satisfied. Let us occasionally take them to the circus and they will be happy. Since men obviously have a natural inclination towards freedom, freedom can be suppressed but not completely abolished. So every repressive regime must from time to time provide safety valves to release the pent-up pressures of aggression it has caused and to keep the barrel from bursting. *Einmal ist keinmal*, it is said, just once doesn't count. This restores hard-learned morality and joyless discipline and renders an oppressive rule more tolerable. The Caesars led the people to the arena where they could work off their desire for blood watching the gladiators fight. Their victims even thanked them for the privilege: 'Ave Caesar, those who are about to die salute you!' Triumphant conquerors at times allowed their soldiers to deride the vanquished with mocking songs. Modern dictators are fond of sponsoring sports events; they subsidize highly trained professionals with whom the people can identify and who can become an object of the people's pride. For the more peace-loving there is stamp collecting, with a wide assortment of special issues in constant supply.

Any drilled-in morality evidently needs occasional suspensions and momentary excesses, if it is to be followed. The church's seasons of fasting are more likely to be observed if they are preceded by an exhausting carnival season. At certain times the medieval church used to rise above its absolute reality and satirized itself, e.g., in the donkey festival, the feast of fools and the Easter laughter. According to Lesskow's story *The Exorcism of the Devil*, a swinging night of dancing followed by a morning of tearful, contrite repentance in the monastery belonged together as a means of elevating life above its boring mediocrity.[3] Temporary suspensions evidently are part of the economy of any regime unreconciled to freedom, of any morality which is at odds with the natural drives of men and of the kind of mental or spiritual reflection which paralyses spontaneous feelings. Thus excesses channelled into games support the normal state of regimentation.

How then do these games work? Their function is to mitigate the burdens which precede and follow them. The modern achievement-centred society has therefore for its own sake widened the scope given to games and free play by extending vacation time. As the term 'vacation' implies, we get away for a while to become better achievers and more willing workers. Conversely, we are not working to enjoy better vacations or to live our lives more freely. The military term 'leave' clearly shows the connection of free time to the service motif. The emphasis in our lives is on service, on our labour. There are other recreational activities as well which serve the purpose of unwinding and of relaxation. Conditioned and regulated man needs his nightly whodunit on television. There he vicariously experiences adventure which has long since vanished from his monotonous world. In the Western hero, the average man in house slippers can see himself once more as an image of virile strength. Tourism supplements a world deprived of experiences with 'the sights and sounds of faraway places'. Colourful posters promise encounters with strange lands and strange customs, but at the camping places and beaches we do in fact meet people exactly like ourselves, and hardly ever does anyone escape his own circles. Tourists are insured, even against rain. Bavarian folk dancers and Hawaiian hula dancers are flown in from Munich or San Francisco. Carnivals flourish more than ever. They become the fraternizing opiate of the masses. 'Every Jack is different', the saying goes in the Rhenish Carnival, but he is different only as 'Jack', not as a human being. One is *different* for a time, but one does not change. We play with alternatives to normal life, since in normal life alternatives have almost ceased to exist.[4]

These areas reserved for free play are of considerable importance to the structures of authority and labour and their respective disciplines and moral systems. They serve as temporary suspensions of the normal state of affairs (the function of suspension)[5] and allow relaxation from everyday tensions and demands (the function of relaxation). But in this process the abnormal state is strictly limited to a supporting role for the normal life situation: the purpose of relaxation is to restore a person's fitness for coming demands. Again, the areas reserved for freedom in vacations and pleasure in the final analysis serve only to strengthen and stabilize labour morale and political obedience. There rarely occurs in this context what Harvey Cox would like to see, namely a festive affirmation of living and an alternative to the daily routine of work, convention and mediocrity.[6] The freedom men seek is preplayed and acted out in insensitive areas; the joy which allows a person to breathe freely becomes a mere tool to compensate for joyless labour. This is abetted by the fact that people have lost their capacity for leisure; they no longer know how to do nothing, since constant and 'full employment' has become their ideal. So they have to 'do something' even with their leisure time. Having mastered their work they have to master their leisure as well. Leisure then becomes a continuation of the rhythm of work by other means. The leisure industry, with good business sense, helps people to find 'something to do' with their leisure. Yet those who would master their leisure merely manage to violate their own freedom. Freedom has a way of coming by itself to those who are open and receptive. Those who feel they must master it are destroying freedom even in their leisure.

So we find, even at first glance, that in our society the familiar preserves of freedom reveal patterns of an alienated way of managing our enjoyment and of an unfree way of dealing with our freedom.

But even an alienated way of dealing with our enjoyment deals with enjoyment. As relief valves for the pressures of everyday failures these games still are games of liberation. They are games of liberation played by those in bondage in support of their own bondage. When Theodor W. Adorno remarks to the point that 'there is no real life in false living', we have to insist that false living is still living. 'A living dog is better than a dead lion' (Eccles. 9.4b).

Games of liberation

Movements of emancipation, particularly those concerned with the 'humanizing emancipation of man', cannot do without the games of freedom merely because these have been and are being abused. Otherwise revolutionary zeal with its ethics of indictment, protest and demand would sanction the very achievement-centred society from which it wants to liberate mankind. The Puritans used to tell their children, 'You haven't come into the world for pleasure'. The Neo-Puritans are saying exactly the same thing. The absence of humane qualities in the old society is causing them to climb the barricades of criticism. But they themselves speak of the humanism of their new society only in terms of an absolute demand. So they get caught between criticism and demand in a 'restless back and forth which seeks reconciliation without finding it', as Hegel has said.[7] With that the last vestiges of the humane are vanishing completely from history.

The history of life's reformations and revolutions has up to now revealed an irritating paradoxical nature: The *Reformation* fought justification by works in the medieval ecclesiastical society with its system of penances, indulgences and almsgiving on the grounds of a new faith which justified without the works of the law. The Reformation also abolished the holidays, games and safety valves of that society. This led to the establishment of the Puritan society of penny pinchers and to the industrial workaday world among the very people who had at first insisted on believing that men are justified by faith alone. Nowhere did the morality of achievement find greater support than in the Protestant countries, Scotland and Swabia, for example.

In Eastern Europe the feudalistic systems of work and pleasure were abolished by *socialist revolutions* which promised people a humanizing liberation, only to establish poor Stachanov as the patron saint of overfilled norms and Prometheus as a pre-revolutionary hero of labour. The socialist revolutions merely managed to fight battles of production with paramilitary labour brigades and to foster a spirit of joyless *tristesse* in the various paradises of the working class. In Prague the 1948 revolution closed down 2,000 coffeehouses, restaurants and beer gardens, the very ones in which the revolution itself had once been debated and plotted during the days of the easy-going Austrian monarchy. Now socialist mass sports have become the new safety valve. So freedom remains under control. If a revival of the creative arts develops in spite of this, as it did in Prague some time ago during the famous Kafka discussions, it immediately constitutes a threat to those who believe that 'trust is good, control is better' (Lenin). As a matter of fact, the opposite alone is true and humane, 'Control is good, trust is better'.

A repressive society cannot be liberated by tightening the safety valves and channeling the pent-up pressures into greater efforts. This merely results in the transformation of one unreconciled society into another. This kind of revolution is 'grandpa's revolution', as the Paris students and Amsterdam demonstrators derisively called it.

To accomplish a *humanizing emancipation* of man in a given society, it makes more sense to wrest control of the alienated games of that society from the ruling interests and to change them into games of freedom which prepare men for a more liberated society. Previous attempts to change the organizational structure of labour have always begun with that very structure and inevitably resulted in yet another organizational structure of labour which in turn seemed just as much in need of change. How would it be if the liberation of man were to begin with the existing game patterns and within the scope of free play currently open to him? This means that leisure time has to be enlarged and that expectations and alternatives for a more humane future have to be tested in those areas where men seek recreation and relaxation. It means that we wrest control of the games from those who have specialized in leisure-time activities and that we stimulate new and greater self-sufficiency. It means that we move from a merely reproductive imagination, which in its leisure recapitulates the rhythm of the working world, to an imagination productive of a more liberated world. Games become hopeless and witless if they serve only to help us forget for a while what we cannot change anyway.

We enjoy freedom when we anticipate by playing what can and shall be different and when in the process we break the bonds of the immutable *status quo*. We find pleasure in games and enjoy the suspended state of playing when the game affords us critical perspectives for change in our otherwise burdensome world. In that case the significance of games is identical with that of the arts, namely to construct 'anti-evironments' and 'counter-environments' (McLuhan)[8] to ordinary and everyday human environments and through the conscious confrontation of these to open up creative freedom and future alternatives. We are then no longer playing merely with the past in order to escape it for a while, but we are increasingly playing with the future in order to get to know it.

Liberation from the bonds of the present system of living takes place by *playing games*. At first this probably always happens quite playfully: We discover with a laugh that things need not at all be as they are and as we have been told they have to be. When the fetters are suddenly removed, we try to walk upright. Just so the games of productive imagination afford us an opportunity to experiment with free expression and with new human relationships. Games, liberties and pleasures have a definite sociopsychological function in contemporary society. We have described that function in terms of suspension, relaxation and compensation and we have found that it has a stabilizing effect in the realm of labour and authority. Conversely, when we are now pleading for games, freedom and enjoyment in their function of preparation and experimentation for a better future, when we advocate games as a means of testing a new life-style, we do not just intend to integrate them again, differently and perhaps better, into the realm of political life. We intend rather to set forth more clearly their liberating effect.

The subculture of *political humour* enjoys its greatest popularity in dictatorships. Political humour distorts the images of the rulers and of their propaganda; its dual meanings and comic situations have a liberating effect. Games, jokes, caricatures, parodies, imitations and intentional misunderstandings may be regarded as a means of emancipation for those who are burdened and heavy-laden. The medieval dances of death served to liberate the people by denuding the privileged classes of their trappings of dignity and their status symbols. Sebastian Brant's *Ship of Fools* had a similarly disarming, reflective effect on the members of a highly respected society. These are the means the powerless use to shake off their yoke, for in these surprise situations they are escaping the bond of fear which has made their yoke possible. The power of the powerless lies in such liberations from fear, in their laughter at the expense of deified rulers who are nothing after all but dolled-up dwarfs. People who are no longer afraid – yet who is really not afraid? – can no longer be ruled with ease, although of course they can be shot. Wise Stoics and Christian martyrs have attempted to demonstrate this in the arena to the tyrants of old. They passed 'through freely', either in the Stoic fashion 'without fear and without hope' or in the Christian manner 'with a hope, where there is no hope'.

The mechanism of fear and of worry always keeps men down on the ground. Freedom begins when men suddenly find themselves to be without fear. The most enduring pillar of all ideologies of absolute rule is most likely the notion that death is the end of everything and that therefore this life, however sad it may be, is all there is. 'Le mort est nécessairement une contre-révolution' appeared on a Paris wall in May of 1958. All liberation movements begin with a few people who are no longer afraid and who begin to act differently from what is expected by those who are threatening them.

> That would suit many a lord just fine ...
> But a resurrection is coming
> It will be quite different from what we expect.
> A resurrection is coming which is
> God's revolution against the lords
> And against the Lord of lords, against death,

wrote Kurt Marti.[9] Here already we find ourselves right at the centre of the game of theology, the liberating game of faith with God against the evil bonds of fear and the grey pressures of care which death has laid upon us. For resurrection faith means courage to revolt against the 'covenant with death' (Isa. 28.15), it means hope for the victory of life which will swallow up and conquer life-devouring death.

3. The theological play of the good will of God

Theology does not have much use for aesthetic categories. Faith has lost its joy, since it has felt constrained to exorcize the law of the old world with a law of the new. Where everything must be useful and used, faith tends to regard its own freedom as good for nothing. It tries to make itself useful and in so doing often gambles away its freedom. Ethics is supposed to be everything. Yet the theological tradition is permeated with aesthetic images and categories. We are going to ease our way into this by starting with questions children ask. It is hard to answer a child's questions when we are no longer children. Still the adult world is unconsciously surrounded by the wondering and repressed questions of childhood.

Why did God create the world?

This is the question of a child who is no longer a child. He has learned that in the adult world everything exists for a good reason; but is there a good reason for the world? At this point the metaphysical way of asking has from its outset encountered the open, the groundless or the abyss. Since Heraclitus it has often used playing as a cosmic world symbol.

'The course of the world is a child at play, moving figures on a board, back and forth; it is the kingdom of a child', says Heraclitus in *Fragment 52* (Diels). That is to say, the primeval becoming has the characteristics of a game. Gods and men appear in the totality of the world, as if they were part of the game. Seemingly at play, the world moves in suspension. Hence, the kingdom belongs to the child.

The philosopher Eugen Fink interprets this world symbol to mean that 'the world is groundless'.[1] 'We can play, precisely because we are open to the world and because in this openness of our human existence there is a certainty about the groundlessness of the governing whole.' Game playing then corresponds to the ultimate groundlessness of the world as the suitable option for man. Since the world does not provide firm ground under our feet, it does – and for that very reason – give us the playground for freedom. Because equilibrium seems to be so uncertain, the figures of the game are movable and the players must be lighthanded and limber. When the heavy burdens of earth pull the players down, they lose their place in the game. We are playing in the world and with the world, and we are trying through free play to make ourselves fit for the totally-other – or we are sinking into the abyss of the world out of fear and are grasping at things which give no hold with sorrow. If there is no firm ground for the world, within which all things are nailed down by grounds and purposes, then the world is either a desert of absurdity or it has to be the game of the totally-other.[2] The world turns into desert where the freedom of play has been lost. 'The world – a gate to thousand deserts, still and cold. He who has lost what thou hast lost has naught to hold'; so sounds the metaphysical complaint of nihilism in the words of Nietzsche. But the *wisdom* of God is saying: 'I was daily his delight, rejoicing [playing] before him always' (Prov. 8.30). This is the wisdom of creation. It does not take the world and life either more seriously or more lightly than creation demands, a creation which is neither divine nor antidivine. Not Atlas carries the burden of the world on his shoulders, but the child is holding the globe in his hands.

Faith answers the unchildish childhood question in a childlike way; and the wisdom of theology ends with the liberty of the children of God. There is no purposive rationale for the proposition that something exists rather than nothing. The existence of the world is not necessary. Theology expresses this with its understanding of the world as 'God's creation'. It reasons as follows: If creation is necessary for God himself, then God is not its 'free creator'. If on the other hand creation is merely an accident or misadventure from eternity, then the free creator is not God but a capricious demon. How then can we explain God's freedom relative to his creation? The world as free creation cannot be a necessary unfolding of God nor an emanation of his being from his divine fullness. God is free. But he does not act capriciously. When he creates something that is not God but also not nothing, then this must have its ground not in itself but in God's *good will or pleasure*. Hence the creation is God's play, a play of his groundless and inscrutable wisdom. It is the realm in which God displays his glory.

But what is this good will of God if it is to provide the *ground* of a groundless world? Good will is a gracious liking commensurate to God and suitable for him. God created the world neither out of his own essence nor by caprice. It did not have to be, but creation suits his deepest nature or else he would not enjoy it. This may be expressed symbolically in the categories of play: 'When we are saying that the creative God plays, we are expressing with this image the metaphysical insight that, although the creation of the world and of man constitutes meaningful divine action, this action is in no way a necessary one.'³ With exactly the same term, 'meaningful but not necessary', Huizinga and many others have also described human play as distinct from productive and gainful labour.

But here theology must insist on a minor distinction. The Old Testament term for the creative activity of God is *bārā*. It is used exclusively to describe divine activity and is never used for the works of men. When we say that the creative God is playing, we are talking about a playing that differs from that of man. The creative God plays with his own possibilities and creates out of nothing that which pleases him. Man can only play with something which, in turn, is playing with him. When man is playing, he is himself at stake in the game and he is also being played with. He cannot play with nothing or a void. He can only play in love. Still there are points of contact. Like the creation, man's games are an expression of freedom and not of caprice, for playing relates to the joy of the creator with his creation and the pleasure of the player with his game. Like creation, games combine sincerity and mirth, suspense and relaxation. The player is wholly absorbed in his game and takes it seriously, yet at the same time he transcends himself and his game, for it is after all only a game. So he is realizing his freedom without losing it. He steps outside himself without selling himself. The symbol of the world as God's free creation out of his good pleasure corresponds to the symbol of man as the child of God. This is what Jesus meant when he turned from his disciples to the children: 'Truly, I say to you, whoever does not receive the kingdom of God like a child shall not enter it' (Mark 10.15). We do not know whether Heraclitus' saying was known in Jesus' time or whether Jesus had heard it. The church fathers, who preserved Heraclitus' sentence for us, found in it a common ground.[4]

For what purpose did God create the world? This is the question of the adult in the child who does not want to play any more but needs goals in order to make something respectable of himself. But the creator God is not *deus faber*. He did not have to create something to realize himself. As we were saying, he has brought forth his creation to enjoy it, to display its splendour and in all things to glorify himself, as the language of tradition puts it. But what does this mean?

The world is *theatrum gloriae Dei*, said the serious-minded Calvin, who at most permitted himself to play a little boccie on Sunday afternoons. The purpose of man's creation, he says in his *Geneva Catechism*, is 'to glorify God'. 'What is the chief end of man?' asks the *Westminster Catechism* of 1647, which the Puritans used to memorize so well, and the answer is: 'Man's chief end is to glorify God and to enjoy Him forever.'[5] It is not man's purpose to 'realize God', as the humanist Ludwig Feuerbach had demanded, who considered 'God' as the ideal of a future mankind. Man is to give glory to the true God and rejoice in God's and his own existence, for this by itself is meaningful enough. Joy is the meaning of human life, joy in thanksgiving and thanksgiving as joy. In a way, this answer abolishes the intent of such questions as: For what purpose has man been created? For what purpose am I here? For the answer does not indicate ethical goals and ideal purposes but justifies created existence as such. The important thing about this answer is precisely the awkward surprise it contains. When we ask, For what purpose do I exist?, the answer does not lie in demonstrable purposes establishing my usefulness but in the acceptance of my existence as such and in what the Dutch biologist and philosopher Buytendijk has called the 'demonstrative value of being'.[6] Recognizing this, we escape the dreadful questions of existence. For what purpose am I here? Am I useful? Can I make myself useful?

In our society the training of children already involves such threatening questions of existence according to which the meaning of life allegedly lies in rendering service, being useful and having purposes. 'Be good for something or you are good for nothing' the beneficiaries of society are saying. When a man sees the meaning of life only in being useful and used, he necessarily gets caught in a crisis of living, when illness or sorrow makes everything including himself seem useless. The catechism question of the 'chief end' of man's life is already a temptation to confuse the enjoyment of God and our existence with goals and purposes. Anyone who lays hold of the joy which embraces the creator and his own existence also gets rid of the dreadful question of existence: For what? He becomes immune to the prevailing ideologies that promise man meaning for life only to abuse him for their own purposes. He becomes immune also to a society which values and rewards men only in terms of their practical usefulness and their suitability as labour and consumers.

It is not self-evident that we should glorify God and rejoice in him if the world seems to us like a desert. The notion that enjoying God implies enjoying our own existence has been obscured by our Puritan training in self-control. Mistrust of our own nature and its drives and of the splendour of nature outside has kept many people from this enjoyment and spoiled it for them. It helps us to get a step further if we accompany the biologists Buytendijk and Portmann through the realm of living things and have a look at nature with a view other than that of a technician. Both have shown that even animal behaviour can be playful. 'To put it simply, the birds are singing much more than Darwin permits', says Buytendijk. In view of the extravagant luxury of specific types, of colourful splendour and hypertelic forms in the world of living things, he contends with Portmann that nature's purpose-free abundance leads the biologist to the concept of self-representation. Nature not only presents a picture of structures serving the preservation of individuals and species, but it also displays its riches, and that is called freedom.[7]

This self-representation of living things or 'demonstrative value of being' ascends through the stages of living things and evidently reaches its preliminary completion in man in proportion to his capabilities. Does this not resemble the world view expressed by Paul in Romans 8, where the longing of the creature groaning in travail is directed towards the revealing of the glorious liberty of the children of God, since even the creature seeks freedom from its bondage to decay? So man is not alone in the desert with his pain, still and cold. His pain reflects the sufferings of the whole creation in bondage. In his liberty, an earnest of which he can grasp by the spirit of adoption as God's child, the creation also finds its liberty. But this is not the freedom of those who exploit nature or of the animal trainer, since that kind of freedom creates enmity rather than community. In what then does the freedom we are talking about consist? Is not man's playful rejoicing in his existence, his pure unforced pleasure in creative play and his fondness for expression and representation exactly that 'demonstrative value of being' of which Buytendijk speaks in reference to animals? In that case man's free self-representation has to be the human echo to the pleasure of God in his creation. The glorification of God lies in the demonstrative joy of existence. In that case man in his uninhibited fondness for this finite life and by his affirmation of mortal beauty shares the infinite pleasure of the creator.

Pallieter, a character in the novel by Felix Timmermans, one day was leaning against a tree with his hands in his pocket, as was his custom, happily watching the play of the rays of the sun in the leaves. Somebody came by and asked, as we are often asked: 'What are you doing there?' And Pallieter answered: 'I am.'[8] Just like that, we too are evidently supposed to be busy with something, as if our existence were justified or rendered beautiful by this. The opposite is true: our existence is justified and made beautiful before we are able to do or fail to do anything. If we are working at something, we have started out from leisure. This is why the Romans used to call work *negotium*, non-leisure. When our labour is successful, joy has already been there at its beginning. Leisure earned by working and self-created joys do not satisfy.

'If man knows himself to be free and desires to use his freedom, then this activity is play,' says Sartre following Schiller. But what is the objective concomitant of this kind of freedom in the world?

The world has to be an *open process* if there is to be hope of man's self-realization and if it is to provide an ultimate home for man's identity (Bloch).[9] Man's hope has as its corollary an openness of the world towards the future. For *homo faber*, who first must fashion himself, since he does not have himself, the world consequently is *laboratorium possibilis salutis*, a laboratory of possible fortune or misfortune. When he himself does the experimenting, he regards the world as his laboratory. When others do the experimenting through him, he regards it as his place of work.

The conception of the *world as history* or as a 'land of unlimited opportunity' is very well suited to the 'not-yet compulsion in the American soul', the Faustian striving and the homelessness of Ahasuerus.[10] As a matter of fact, men find themselves suffering, hoping and working in an open history. But in what and before what can that open history itself be found? In the universe of nature or in the void or in God? Men are standing *in* history, but history itself is contained in a totally-other. This is not the other of nature which men have been *making their own* in the course of history. It is the totally-other before which men, in the course of that history, have sought to *represent* themselves. The human element in labour and the production of food, in social patterns and cultural expressions, always involves self-representation.[11] All things men use always contain in their respective processes an expression of the *demonstrative value of being*. Whenever man produces something, he demonstrates himself as well, even if only by a small individualistic departure from the work rules. He presents and represents himself and, in a manner of speaking, answers a call with his presence. This self-representation is not identical with self-realization by labour, for the creative play of expression does not depend on successes and accomplishments, although it does not preclude these.

Theologically speaking, *creation aims at history*, as the Old Testament clearly indicates. But it also aims *history at the new creation*, as the prophets and the New Testament have shown. Freedom does not only press towards its realization but towards representation and celebration as well. Freedom needs more than to be *realized*, it must be celebrated. If with Sartre we may call free activity or the activity of free men a 'play', then we must consider the world – as its objective concomitant – the 'play area' of that freedom. The world is groundless and bottomless, and precisely for that reason a free zone for the liberty of playing creatively with correspondences to the totally-other God. So the stakes in the game are not realizations, successes and accomplishments but the endless beauties and liberties of the finite concomitants of the infinite joy of the creator.

The moral and political *seriousness of making history* and of historical struggles is then being suspended by a *calm rejoicing in existence* itself. This does not make seriousness superfluous. Rather it preserves and protects it against the demonic, against despair, against man's self-deification and self-vilification, against the mania of perfection and of despondency in the face of imperfection. Our social and political tasks, if we take them seriously, loom larger than life. Yet infinite responsibility destroys a human being because he is only man and not god. I have an idea that laughter is able to mediate between the infinite magnitude of our tasks and the limitations of our strength. Many people, who really get down to work, are saying – and rightly so: 'Unless we do a lot of joking, we have to cry and cannot get anything done.'

World as history is of necessity the symbol of *homo faber*. *Play as a world symbol* does contain archaic conceptions but goes beyond the idea of world as history, if we extend this concept to the eschatology of being and do not confine ourselves to the early stages of human thought. Play as world symbol goes beyond the categories of doing, having and achieving and leads us into the categories of being, of authentic human existence and demonstrative rejoicing in it. It emphasizes the creative against the productive and the aesthetic against the ethical. Earthbound labour finds relief in rejoicing, dancing, singing, and playing. This also does labour a lot of good.

The creative playing of men is always a playing with something which, in turn, plays with the player. Man plays with the waves of the ocean and they play with him. He plays with colours, sounds and words and also becomes their playmate. He speaks and responds, is active and passive, giving and receiving at once. Playing he is neither master nor servant. This is true not only for games *in* life but also for the game *of* life. 'The further we progress in the analysis of existence,' writes Buytendijk, 'the clearer it becomes . . . that man also has the possibility of being played with rather than playing, of being the one who is sheltered by the game. This leads to a mysterious transformation. Man becomes aware that the encompassing, loving ground of his existence is playing a wondrous game with him. It is – as the poet Charles Péguy has shown us – the game of *Qui perd gagne*, the loser wins.'[12]

It is indeed annoying and strange that the book of Job, which tells of the tortures of an innocently suffering righteous man, sets his fate into the framework of a heavenly wager between God and Satan and that Goethe's *Faust* also begins with a prologue in heaven.[13] Is the intent here to offset the insatiable restlessness of

Faust and even the irrelievable suffering of Job by playing a game? But Charles Péguy means even more than that. He evidently means the game of grace in which the loser wins and the lost are saved, the poor are filled and the rich are left empty-handed; the game of eschatological surprises in which the 'first shall be the last and the last first'. To comprehend this game of all-reversing grace may well require that we have to give up the last vestige of pride in our own achievements and free ourselves of selfishness and self-pity so that we may join in an affirmation of grace, full of wonder. This brings us to the core of our next question.

Why did God become man?

Why, of all people, Jesus of Nazareth? – This is the question of faith hungering for understanding and of understanding which cannot decide for faith without good reason. Did God have to become man to reconcile his justice with his mercy, his holiness with his love? Did man's sin make the coming of the redeemer necessary? And if that is the case, why did he wait to come at that particular time and did he come, of all places, to that particular corner of the world? asked the pagan philosopher Celsus. Why did God not manifest himself in many bodies at the same time? It is not usually in the nature of the idea to realize itself in a single individual, said Celsus' successors Lessing and David Friedrich Strauss.

Theological tradition has insisted on the necessity of the incarnation as a remedy for man's sin. By describing the misery into which man has fallen, theology provides the negative matrix for an understanding of redemption from misery. Uncovering the needs of men, it seeks to establish the necessity for the redeemer who turns away man's need. While this enabled tradition to explain why God *had to* become man, it failed to make clear why he *wanted* to become man and why it is specifically Jesus of Nazareth by whom this turning of all human need has been accomplished. There remains in the story of Jesus an irreducible historical contingency which cannot be reconstructed by theological systems. But this random element in the historical sphere points to the freedom of God within the polarity of man's need and divine redemption from that need. The other area in which the biblical word-group of *good will* has been used is therefore the presentation of events related to the birth, baptism and transfiguration of Jesus. The word-group of *glory*, which denotes a similar content, occurs beyond this in the narratives of Jesus' resurrection. This indicates that God has no compelling reasons to become man in Jesus of Nazareth and to turn away man's need. Yet in his infinite love he is *well-pleased* to do just that.

Again, we may ask, is not then God's action caprice and are not the pronouncements of faith capricious claims? But between the extremes of *necessity and caprice* there is still another possibility. Even if the revelation of God in Jesus Christ is not necessary for God himself, it does not constitute caprice; rather it corresponds to God's deepest nature. Since this revelation 'co-responded' to God's deepest nature and even the contradiction of Jesus' crucifixion corresponds to God's love for the lost, faith calls him 'son'. God was not compelled by human misery to come in the flesh, but he came because of his own free and uncaused love. In this love God does not merely react to the misery of his creatures but creates something new for them as well. The story of Christ must not be understood as a mere emergency measure on God's part relieving the present need and restoring the ancient play of creation. While the misery of the beloved does indeed prompt God's love to be merciful in the measure of man's need, God's love goes beyond his mercy and beyond man's misery. So it reaches beyond the mere restoration of the sick to the healthy state of a new life. The sinner needs the redeemer, but the redeemer comes of his own free will and thus he guides us through misery and its redemption to a liberated future which he himself is bringing about. The new creation arising from redemption is not just the restored or repaired old creation; it is a new one also in reference to the first creation. It is a new game. Sin is not a stain on the white vest of mankind being washed away. As Luther has observed correctly, it is not sin which must leave man, but man who must leave sin. This does not happen by repairing man's mistakes or restoring his health; it occurs when man dies to the law, to sin and to death and awakens to new life. In Paul, therefor,e grace has become *abundant* where sin once had ruled; it is not merely a matter of divine reparations.

So we may well point to God as the *one necessary* to change our human condition of need, but we cannot really talk about God in Christ unless we proceed from God's freedom which is love. We

The First Liberated Men in Creation

should not talk of God unless we have to, said Bultmann quite correctly. But we can talk of God only if God himself begins the talking, Karl Barth contended, perhaps still more correctly. It is one thing to discover the *need* which makes talking of God necessary; the *freedom* to talk of God in that situation is quite another matter. This freedom is being offered by God alone. Theology therefore is both necessary and unnecessary. It has relevance for men in the realms of need and necessity. Yet it springs from man's wonder at the story of Christ and from his rejoicing in the uncaused grace of God of which its speaks. In that wonder the realm of liberty is already entering the realm of need and necessity and bursting its chains. On first glance *Christian theology* is indeed the *theory of a practice* which alleviates human need: the theory of preaching, of ministries and services. But on second glance Christian theology is also an abundant rejoicing in God and the *free play* of thoughts, words, images and songs with the grace of God. In its one aspect it is the theory of a practice, in the other it is pure theory, i.e., a point of view which transforms the viewer into that which he views, hence *doxology*. The freedom to talk with God and of God is being opened by God's joy. It cannot be forced. For true awareness cannot be coercive; it does not come about by either authoritarian pressure or the force of logic. It presupposes liberty. Being aware of God is an art and – if the term may be permitted – a noble game.

If the history of God with Christ and through him with suffering mankind arises from the good will of God and if God's freedom, even in the history of salvation, cannot be reconstructed in terms of a purposeful rational system, how then can we understand this history by means of the aesthetic categories of play?

Jesus is said to have wept, but there is no mention of a laughing Jesus in spite of Harvey Cox's *Playboy* article.[14] On the other hand, the dogmatic tradition – quite without humour – has used this to deduce the sinlessness of Jesus: *risu abstinuit*, he never laughs! Yet the Old Testament psalmist expected of redeemed existence: 'Then our mouth was filled with laughter.'

According to Luke, while at the birth of the child in the manger presentient angels of God are singing praises, under his *cross* at Golgotha there are only insensitive soldiers playing dice over his garments, having first ridiculed him as a harlequin and king of thorns by order of their superiors. The life of Jesus in the gospels stands under the signs of manger and cross, homelessness and murder. In the face of such suffering, aesthetic categories fail rather abruptly. It is difficult to consider the sufferings of the forsaken Christ and his pain of death a serious loving game of God for man's benefit – as the mystics occasionally have done. It is also difficult to explain the history of the cross in terms of God's cunning betrayal of the devil, as theologians of the ancient church have on occasion attempted. At this point the categories of play seem misplaced. The language of the gospels tends towards expressions from the realms of slavery, labour and suffering. As the Philippian *hymnus* is saying, he gave up his play of being equal with God and took the form of a servant and became obedient unto death on a cross. Believers say that he, who took upon himself this form of a servant, has had sorrow and labour with their sins. The liberated are saying that not by his happy life, but by his wounds, have we been healed.

So Hugo Rahner slides into a gnostic-docetic way of thinking when he says: 'What at the surface appears as fate, as suffering, or – in the Christian sense – as participation in the seemingly senseless destruction of the cross, is for the mystic, whose vision penetrates all veils, the wondrously conceived game of an eternal love, a game so painstaking and manifold in its conception that only love could have devised it.'[15] Can we really talk about the cross of Jesus just as a 'veil' of suffering, tortured flesh through which we can see a pleasant sky illuminated by the brilliant rays of the sun of God's love? I think we should literally and sincerely leave the cross out of the game. In spite of Bach, the dying agonies of Jesus do not fit the categories of song. Though we must not understand his death as a tragedy in the classical sense, still Jesus did not die as a 'fool'. After all, Golgotha was not Oberammergau.

Easter is an altogether different matter. Here indeed begins the laughing of the redeemed, the dancing of the liberated and the creative game of new, concrete concomitants of the liberty which has been opened for us, even if we still live under conditions with little cause for rejoicing. Harvey Cox with his image of 'Christ as Harlequin'[16] should have taken the cross more seriously to awaken the spirit of festivity and the joy of imagination from the vantage point of the resurrection. Jesus' death was no joke. Those who are aware of God in the cry of the forsaken Jesus have abandoned naïve religious games with the gods. Yet through his death and by virtue of his resurrection 'death has become a mockery', as Luther was able to say – although, of course, death is still here. Awareness of the resurrection of Christ calls forth in the believer a mocking attitude towards 'the world with its great wrath' (Paul Gerhardt). Since ancient times Easter hymns have been rejoicing in the victory of life by exorcistically laughing at death, making a mockery of hell and provoking the rulers of this world. The Easter hymn in I Corinthians 15.55–7 is an early example:

> 'Death is swallowed up in victory.'
> 'O death, where is thy victory?
> O death, where is thy sting?' . . .
> But thanks be to God, who
> gives us the victory through
> our Lord Jesus Christ.

Even in the days of Protestant orthodoxy, which is well-known for its dryness, Easter sermons used to begin with a joke.[17] Laughter takes away the seriousness of an attack and debases it. It displays an unassailable freedom and superiority precisely at the point where the powers and rulers of this world have been reckoning with fear and guilt feelings. And when the partner of these powers and rulers is death, Easter indeed becomes the beginning of the rebellion of the liberated against the bonds of their slavery. Their rebellion does not have its origins in an ethical imperative but in the grateful rejoicing of liberty itself. It is transmorally grounded in the resurrection faith.

Easter begins with *celebration*, for Easter is the feast where the resurrected Christ makes a thank-offering in gratitude for his resurrection and breaks bread with his disciples. At first, in early Christianity, the epiphanies of Easter and the celebration of the Lord's Supper were joined together. The resurrected Christ, as the leader of life against death, initiates his own into the new life and imparts himself to them in the Lord's *Supper*. Therefore the Eucharist is filled with remembrances of the cross and with hope for the new creation. In the unity of remembrance and hope Easter is a demonstration of present rejoicing in grace. It means resurrection, freedom and joy. But Easter is the resurrection of the crucified Christ. It does not overcome the story of Christ's passion so that we need no longer remember it. Rather, it establishes Christ's cross as a saving event. The one who goes *before us* into the glorious and liberated future of God's resurrected is also the one who died for us on the cross. We come face to face with the glory of the coming God beholding the features of the crucified and not through infinite demands or flights of fancy. His degradation leads to our exaltation. His descent into hell opens the heaven of liberty for those in bondage. So the cross of Christ remains the symbol of hope on earth for those who have been liberated.

This is reflected also in their own lives. The Easter life becomes a free hymn of praise to the Father in the midst of the sighing of creation in bondage (Rom. 8). In the midst of creation groaning in travail the children of God display an unsuspected freedom, which makes them cry Abba! Father! in spite of everything. They really have no reason for this at all, except for their fellowship with Christ. Yet in that fellowship the 'power of the resurrection' is always bound up with the 'fellowship of Christ's sufferings', and conversely so. Thus the earnest of the new creation in the spirit of our freedom to believe leads us deeper than ever into solidarity with the sufferings of the world. So the 'power of the resurrection', as Paul calls freedom, makes us followers of the crucified and leads us into fellowship with the forsaken whose brother the crucified has become. This may sound like a contradiction but is in fact an inescapable correlation. Only those who are capable of joy can feel pain at their own and other people's suffering. A man who can laugh can also weep. A man who has hope is able to endure the world and to mourn. Where freedom is near, the chains begin to hurt. Where the Kingdom of God is at hand, we feel the abyss of God-forsakenness. Where men are able to love because they are loved, they are also able to suffer, accept suffering, and live with the dead.

Life as *rejoicing* in liberation, as *solidarity* with those in bondage, as *play* with reconciled existence, and as *pain* at unreconciled existence demonstrates the Easter event in the world.

But can believers play? Don't they have more important things to do? Games always presuppose innocence. Only the innocent, namely children, or those liberated from guilt, namely the beloved, are able to play. The guilty man is at odds with himself. He has lost his spontaneity and cannot play well. Because he disagrees with himself, wavering between self-assertion and self-hatred, he is neither a good loser nor a good winner. The guilty man blackmails himself with an image of what he is not. He is therefore also open to blackmail. Faith is a new spontaneity and a light heart. In faith we accept ourselves as we are and gain new confidence in ourselves because we have been trusted more than we deserve and ever thought possible. The meaning of Easter lies in liberation from the compelling force of guilt and the compulsion to repeat evil. Easter opens up the boundary-crossing freedom to play the game of the new creation. This is possible and meaningful because there is a hell and a hopelessness, which Christ's death has conquered once and for all and which for those who are liberated has been put into the past. The cross of Christ therefore does not belong to the game itself, but it makes possible the new game of freedom. He suffered that we may laugh again. He died that we may live as liberated human beings. He descended into the hell of the forsaken to open for us the heaven of freedom. He became a slave of the enslaved, a servant of those in servitude that these may become free lords of all things.

Resurrection and *Easter freedom* have the cross of Christ behind them, and the physical end of the law, of regimentation and death in the world, still before them. So Easter freedom does not permit us to escape from the world or to forget about it. Rather it leads us critically to accept the world situation with its unacceptable moments and *patiently to bring about change in the world* so that it may become a place of freedom for men. Thus both the laughter of Easter and the sorrow of the cross are alive in liberated men. They are not only laughing with those who laugh and weeping with those who weep, as Paul proposes in Romans 12.15, but they are also laughing with the weeping and weeping with the laughing as the Beatitudes of Jesus recommended. Their game always points critically at the oppressors. It therefore constantly provokes harassment by those who prohibit laughter because they fear liberty.

The end of the history of Christ is then again filled with rejoicing in the good will of God and with the games of liberated mankind. Only history itself is dead serious. Hugo Rahner, following the example set by the Greek doctrine of virtue, liked to talk about a *serious-merry* play. With this middle-of-the-road orientation he probably still remains outside the gates of the history of Christ.

The dialectic of the crucifixion and resurrection of Christ does not lend itself either to an understanding in the Platonic mood of the mean between seriousness and mirth or to the wisdom of Solomon which insists that God must be taken seriously but everything else lightly and with a sense of humour. In the cross of Christ God is taking man dead-seriously so that he may open up for him the happy freedom of Easter. God takes upon himself the pain of negation and the Godforsakenness of judgment to reconcile himself with his enemies and to give to the godless fellowship with himself. Apart from this harsh theological dialectic of death and life, heaven and hell, destruction and reconciliation, anthropological and religious game theories always end up close to the edge of faddism and snobbism. Since they do not take death seriously, life does not really get into the game of freedom.

'It's all *for nothing* anyway,' says the nihilist and falls into despair. 'It's really all *for nothing*,' says the believer, rejoicing in the grace which he can have for nothing and hoping for a new world in which all is available and may be had *for nothing*. 'Ho, every one who thirsts, come to the waters; and he who has no money, come, buy and eat! Come, buy wine and milk without money and without price,' so the prophets of the Old and the New Testaments promise (Isa. 55.1; Rev. 22.17).

What is the ultimate purpose of history?

This is the question of *homo faber* in whose world of labour everything must have a purpose and for whom the purposeless is the senseless and therefore evil. So his idol, *deus faber*, must be a god who reveals his purposes for his history.

But is the question of the ultimate purpose of history really the question of eschatology? To think eschatologically is to think a matter through to its end. Is there at the end of things, of men and of history such a final purpose?

If at the end of all things here is an attainable purpose, it would seem better never to fulfil that purpose, for fulfilment of that purpose renders all of life purposeless. An infinite search for truth is then preferable to possession of the infinite truth. Eschatology as contemplation of the end is then a cunning method of warding off and ever postponing the end so that – as end – it can always provide illumination for that which precedes it. Would not life in history stagnate if it had fulfilled its purpose? Life which is made meaningful by purposes and goals must find the vision of heaven terrible, since that vision only invites infinite and purposeless boredom.

Christian eschatology has never thought of the end of history as a kind of retirement or pay day or accomplished purpose, but has regarded it totally without purpose as a hymn of praise for unending joy, as an ever-varying round dance of the redeemed in the trinitarian fullness of God, and as the complete harmony of soul and body. It has not hoped for an unearthly heaven of bodyless souls but for a new body penetrated by the spirit and redeemed from the bondage of law and death. Christian eschatology has never painted the joy of existing in the new, redeemed, and liberated creation in colours of this life damaged by trouble, labour, and guilt, but it has painted it in colours which for all of us – in Ernst Bloch's beautiful phrase – 'shine back into our childhood', namely the colours of unhindered laughter, devoted vision of the marvellous riches and goodness of God and of new innocence. Christian eschatology has painted the end of history in the colours of aesthetic categories.

This does not mean that at the end of his laborious development man reverts back *to* childhood. Infantilism is no solution for his problems. It does mean, however, that he becomes *like* a child. This is the future of *homo faber*. To be sure, the end of history is a *novum* which has to be *totaliter aliter*, altogether different, if it is to arise from this life with its ever-growing need for redemption. But it will not suffice merely to deny what we now and here experience as negative. The analogies for the indescribable totally-other are therefore taken from the life of childhood which precedes the world of *homo faber*. The images for the coming new world do not come from the world of struggle and victory, of work and achievement, of law and its enforcement, but from the world of primal childhood trust. In Kierkegaard too, on the level of 'religious existence' there is a return of patterns and relationships taken from 'aesthetic existence' and not from 'ethical existence'. They return here in transmoral fashion.

The relation of this life to death and to eternal life is understood in the same way. Life is not a struggle but a prelude, not preparatory labour but a preview of the future life of rejoicing. The elements of perishable time, which – as projection of the future –

abide in eternity, are found in the moments of grace and faith, of joy and love, of openness and hope, and not in the moments of glory due to achievements and efforts. The grace of God in the new creation, which enters and precedes human history, does not spiritualize or moralize but rather embodies itself in the unconscious grace, the charm and loveliness of a living person such as Dostoevski describes in the figure of the whore Sonia.

Since about the sixth century Christian art has been acquainted with a type of dance called the *resurrection dance*. Here, in a spirally round dance, the elevated Christ draws the redeemed upwards towards the Father with a sweep of his mantle. This represents an exact counter-image of the later medieval dances of death in which the sickle bearer is leading emperor, pope, noble, peasant and serf into the pit. The risen one, who opens up the eschatology of freedom, is himself the 'lead dancer in the mystical round', as Hippolytus has said, and the church is his 'bride who dances along'.

In the Christian way of thinking, the so-called final purpose of history is then no purpose at all. It is the liberation of life which the law had made subject to purposes and achievements, to the all-quickening joy of God. The *history of the passion of the world* – and that, speaking with Walter Benjamin, is one of the really viable categories in universal history[18] – has no purpose and does not lead to a theodicy (vindication of divine justice). Its end is its completion in the resurrection of crippled and abused bodies to their glorification in the joy of God. The tortured question in suffering and dying, *Why?*, reveals its dignity in that it does not permit an explanation. It can be answered only by a new creation in which there shall be neither mourning nor crying nor pain, for the former things have passed away (Rev. 21.4). The passion of Christ in the midst of the world's passion ending in the resurrection of the one whom the world crucified is the incarnate assurance of the dawn of that other history of joy in the very midst of the world's unanswered suffering.

Only through our experience of the history of the world as a history of passion do we become painfully aware of the moments of this future which as preview, foretaste and prelude of a totally-other reaches into our mortal life. For this reason we find pain and happiness, suffering and love, hope and mourning, so closely tied together that one cannot be without the other. Men are crying out of conflict between love and pain, hope and mourning, faith and protest. They are crying, not for results, but for redemption to freedom. So at the 'end of history' there awaits us again what has determined its beginnings and accompanied it along the way: pleasure in the play which unites the free God with liberated men. Then men shall 'play with heaven and earth, the sun and all the creatures', says Luther. 'All creatures shall have their fun, love and joy, and shall laugh with thee and thou with them, even according to the body.'[19]

The Christian contemplation of the end, however, has been concerned not only with the *future* but also with *eternity*. For those of us who live in rapidly accelerating times the term 'eternity' has become extremely difficult to comprehend. Eternity sounds like timelessness and lifelessness. Eternity seems to stem from the Greek world view, where the gods lived in eternity but men in passing time. In a world which is not yet complete, where there is still laughing and weeping, eternity may indeed be understood as a future state which is present now without ceasing to be future. Conversely, eternity is a now which is always more than a mere now.[20] In this sense we experience eternity in rejoicing. For in joy the highest form of time experience is its intensity. To make it sound banal: 'A happy man knows neither time nor hour,' as the saying goes. In the jubilant language of hymnody this becomes 'ceaseless joy'. Eternity in this kind of experience is *un*ending, since of rejoicing there can 'be no end'. Time, on the other hand, is an experience of suffering. It is an eternity-experience of pain. Pain says, Does it never end? So pain becomes endless. There is quite a difference between the things we call 'unending' and those we call 'endless'. The joy we call 'heavenly', which points us towards scarcely imaginable 'joys of heaven', has the flavour of eternity. The pains of hell, on the other hand, are not properly called 'eternal' but merely endless. In our experience, therefore, eternity and time are not two categories separating the worlds, but they are categories related to joy and pain. So it makes sense to hope for eternity when it is said: 'Thou dost show me the path of life; in thy presence there is fullness of joy, in thy right hand are pleasures for evermore' (Ps. 16.11). The man who through suffering is aware of the endlessness of time can love eternity of which he has received a foretaste in unending joy.

Is God beautiful?

The modern theological dictionaries have little to say about the 'glory of God' and the 'glorification of man'. The Catholic *Lexikon für Theologie und Kirche* refers to an article entitled 'The Honour of God' which argues with judicial precision that God does not selfishly grasp for his own honour. The Protestant *Religion in Geschichte und Gegenwart*, in its article on 'honour', deals only with the honour of men. Yet *kabod* and *doxa* are key words in the Old and New Testaments.

Karl Barth was the only theologian in the continental Protestant tradition who has dared to call God 'beautiful'.[21] 'God loves us as the one who in his Godhead is lovely or worthy of love. That is what we are saying, when we assert that God is beautiful.' Barth talks about the beauty of God to explain the glory of God. 'We must not fail to recognize that God is glorious in such a way that he radiates joy; so everything he is, he is never apart from beauty, but in beauty.' What does this contribute to our understanding of the glory of God?

In our conventional understanding *God's dominion* is clearly related to the *obedience of men*. Jesus' lordship is demonstrable because and insofar as men are willing to obey him. But in this understanding of dominion and obedience God's dominion becomes an ethical principle which is represented only by the sincerity of an ethical existence either in obedience or in protest. Does this emphasis on a new obedience really conform to the liberty which – according to St Paul – has set free all who are enslaved by the law?

The concept which in biblical usage complements that of God's dominion is the *glory of God*. It is God's display of splendour, his beauty and his kindness or loveliness. On man's side, the corresponding terms are amazement, adoration and praise; that is, freedom which expresses itself in gratitude, enjoyment and pleasure in the presence of beauty. Another corresponding term is love, a love which does not merely manifest itself ethically in love to the neighbour but also aesthetically in festive play before God.

The one-sided emphasis on the dominion of God in the Western church, especially in Protestantism, has subjected Christian existence to judicial and moral categories. Theology describes

Christ as prophet, priest and king, but of doxology and the 'transfiguration of Christ', which is of central importance to the Eastern church, little has remained. The aesthetic categories of the new freedom have given way to the moral categories of the new law and the new obedience. There are many who argue all too hastily that if faith liberates us from the law, from guilt and godless bonds, then *freedom from* is not enough; we must discover the *for what of freedom* as well. So they are searching for new laws and goals of action. But Paul has said in Galatians 5.1, 'For freedom Christ has set us free', and not for a new set of laws. This liberation for freedom is not just a liberation from an old law to a new one, but also a liberation from the compulsion and coercion to act in the first place. We are not merely set free from an old, alien law, but we are, so to speak, set free even from the law of our own liberty. This freedom from the coercion to act manifests itself as festive *rejoicing in freedom*.

In the Old Testament tradition the term 'glory of God' is used in association with special theophanies and has a specific meaning.[22] It describes an awareness both of the *fear of Yahweh* and the *glory of Yahweh*. Hence the *kabod* of Yahweh has pronounced mystic traits. Psalm 97 tells of the glory of God in thunder, lightning and all-consuming fire. In the prophet Ezekiel it appears as storm, cloud, lightning and the roar of water. The redacted priestly tradition takes it to be a glowing fiery substance. In each case it is something men cannot bear. 'For man shall not see me and live' (Exod. 33.20). Therefore Moses is asked to hide in the cleft of a rock, when he is chosen to behold the back of the passing *beauty of Yahweh* and to remain alive (Exod. 33). After his encounter with God on the mountain, his face reveals an unbearable brightness which frightens the people of Israel so that he has to cover it with a veil. If in the Old Testament the 'glory of God' can be called beautiful, then it is only in the sense of the religious poet Rilke's *Duineser Elegien*: 'For the beautiful is nothing but the beginning of the terrible, which we are just barely able to endure; and we admire it so because it calmly refuses to destroy us.' The Hebrew traditions never attached special importance to events of this kind. After all, they cannot be repeated. The records of these encounters with God consistently stressed the 'word of God' rather than the visible circumstances in which they 'happened'. But when the prophets *pro*claimed the coming dominion of God in words of judgment and promise, all these words of God, which destroy history and announce future, were in the last analysis taken by them as signs of a visible theophany of God, that is of the glory of God with which all the earth shall be filled. The historical words declaring God's will as law and comfort point to God's ultimate and universal glorification, when he himself shall dwell among us in the new creation. Hearing the word of God then points to the final vision of his glory which is to come. The *hope for a vision of God* has its roots not only in the Greek tradition but – in this eschatological sense – in the Hebrew tradition as well. Then no man will have to teach another. For they shall all see him as he is, face to face, says Jeremiah 31.34.

In the New Testament also, *doxa* signifies divine honour, divine splendour, divine power and visible divine brightness. The term '*doxa*' describes both the divinity of the father and the divinity of the son. By the *doxa* of the father Jesus is resurrected from shameful death (Rom. 6.4). God has raised him from the dead and given him the glory (1 Peter 1.21). While in the Old Testament the glory of God is the epitome of the anticipated future of God, the resurrection of the crucified from the dead signifies his resurrection into that very future. The pronouncements about God's glory may therefore be applied to Jesus as well. Since he has been raised into the glory of the coming God, that glory has already entered the sufferings of this time through him and through his fate. Since he has been raised into God's future, that future in turn has already come into the present through him. Therefore the 'lord of glory' (I Cor. 2.8) also stands for the 'God of glory' (Acts 7.2). The brightness of divine glory is reflected in the face of Christ and illuminates the hearts of men through him, just as on the first day of creation the creator 'let light shine out of darkness' (II Cor. 4.6).

In the Synoptic Gospels divine brightness appears at the birth and transfiguration of Jesus. In other passages dealing with the earthly life of Jesus the Synoptics rarely use the term, reserving it rather for the manifestations of the risen Christ. Only John identifies the exalted Christ completely with the earthly Jesus and speaks of the *doxa* of the earthly Jesus as well. While he too regards awareness of the glory of Jesus as a matter of faith and not of direct sight, still such faith paradoxically sees the glory of Christ in his suffering and death: The crucifixion of Jesus in shame *is* his glory. His degradation is his exaltation. This means that God has glorified himself in him who has become the servant of all; he has revealed his unbearable brightness in him who died the death of the forsaken for the forsaken; he has shown his honour by making the shame of Jesus on the cross his own shame. This implies a radical shift in our understanding of the glory of God. Masters surround themselves with the splendour of their riches, kings with the honour of their authority, even nations with their glory. But God reveals his strength in the weak, his honour, in lowliness and his splendour in the cross of Christ. His glory is not the splendour of otherworldly superior power but the beauty of love which empties itself without losing itself and forgives without giving itself away. If then the glory of God manifests its brightness on this earth in the face of him who was crucified by its laws and powers, it follows that this law and these powers no longer are glorious and need no longer be feared or adored. He who in the world's view has been disgraced by death on the gallows as a common criminal has then been changed into the one who is most highly exalted. The *glory of the crucified God* leads of necessity to a transformation of all values and takes away the glory from those who have proclaimed themselves divine.

Faith owes its liberty to the awareness of this *crucified God*. In the crucified Christ it recognizes the divine right of grace which justifies those who have no rights. In him it also becomes aware of the creative love of God which makes the ugly lovable. Hence, it recognizes in him also the beauty of God which gives joy to those who mourn. So the hope of faith points to full participation in the glory of God. Just as the believer is justified by 'faith for faith' (Rom. 1.17), he is also being changed 'from glory to glory' (II Cor. 3.18). When by faith he lifts his head from the dust because salvation is near, he also reflects the glory of God 'with unveiled face' (II Cor. 3.18) and need no longer cover himself for fear or shame. He is filled with the 'hope of glory' (Col. 1.27). Dogmatic tradition denotes the justification of the godless as the beginning of their glorification and their glorification as the fulfilment of their justification.

But what do we mean by the *glorification of man?* The First Epistle of John has pointed out that 'it does not yet appear what we shall be, but we know that when he' – namely God himself – 'appears we shall be like him' (I John 3.2). Being a child of God by faith then means being equal with God. This does not imply an apotheosis of man, where man puts himself into God's place, but it does mean man's ultimate transformation to complete conformity with the visible God by seeing him face to face. It is the hope of the Christian faith that the *eritis sicut Deus* of the serpent in the Garden of Eden will actually be fulfilled – but on God's initiative. What is meant here is not just a restoration of man's pure creaturehood, but beyond this a much closer fellowship with God of which we have a foretaste on earth in the fellowship with Christ. Paul states emphatically that he is not merely speaking in a spiritual sense when he talks about the transformation of our 'lowly body' into the new 'glorious body' (Phil. 3.21).

If after this brief excursion into the biblical use of the language about *glory* we now return to the problem of the *relation between ethics and aesthetics*, we must note that these are inseparable both in our awareness of God and in the life of faith. We experience God's dominion equally as his glory and as his beauty and as his sovereignty. His glory cannot be reduced to his dominion and his dominion cannot be reduced to his glory. One interprets the other and protects it from misunderstandings. The beautiful in God is what makes us rejoice in him. So, in corresponding to him and answering him, man's obedience is joined together with his 'new son'. Without the free play of imagination and songs of praise the new obedience deteriorates into *legalism*. Christian living would become a matter of watching out for things one is not allowed to do. But without concrete obedience – which means without physical, social and political changes – the lovely songs and celebrations of freedom become empty phrases. 'We have no right to chant in the Gregorian mode if we fail to cry out for the Jews,' Bonhoeffer justifiably reproached the church at a time when the Hitler regime was persecuting the Jews and the church had inwardly emigrated into liturgy. Yet Bonhoeffer himself was very fond of chanting in the Gregorian mode. Perhaps he was so outraged and cried out against the plight of the silenced Jews because he wanted to sing with them in freedom.

But it is said, 'Man shall not see me [God] and live' (Exod. 33.20). 'It is a fearful thing to fall into the hands of the living God' (Heb. 10.31). So we can 'see' God only by dying to him and being born out of him to new life. Where the believing fellowship with Christ means being baptized into his death, it carries out that dying. Where the believing fellowship with Christ means living with him, the rebirth of hope anticipates that seeing. The glorification of man begins with his awareness of God's justifying love. So the believer is already seeing God, but he is seeing him in the mode of hope and return. Taking part in Christ's visible suffering in the world, the believer shares in Christ's invisible glory. When a man so 'dies' and loses his life, he is seeing God. From the Christian point of view it may therefore be justified to turn Rilke's verse around, awful though this may sound: 'For the terrible is but the beginning of beauty.'

The *vision of God* comes to life by following the crucified with permanent *repentance* and through constant *changing* of existing conditions. It cannot be obtained apart from this. Permanent repentance is the daily dying of the old man and the renewal of the inner, the new man. This is painful but constitutes only the reverse side of rejoicing in hope. Transfiguration cannot be demonstrated on a mountain away from the world. Even the transfiguration of Jesus took place on the road to Jerusalem and the cross. The transfiguration of the unveiled face must be demonstrated in a suffering and struggling transformation which involves changing oneself and existing conditions so that man, together with other men, may be conformed to his future.

Even if the practice of transfiguration and of the vision of God is repentance and change in the footsteps of Christ, they are not painful efforts which we must force ourselves to endure. *Repentance is joy*, as Julius Schniewind has exegetically shown us.[23] Man is not liberated from his old nature by imperatives to be new and to change, but he rejoices in the new which makes him free and lifts him beyond himself. Where repentance is understood as a spiritual return to the evil and rejected past, it deals in self-accusation, contrition, sackcloth and ashes. But when repentance is a return to the future, it becomes concrete in rejoicing, in new self-confidence and in love. Even then we may happen to be mourning, but we can accept the past without loss of identity since we can be another person and have moved beyond ourselves. The journey of Henry IV to Canossa was no repentance. The Occidental tradition of repentance placed too much emphasis on the dying of the old man and thus became legalistic – and not only in the church. It has been unable to demonstrate either practically or theoretically the gospel of the joy of God and the liberation of man. But if repentance as return to the future already is rejoicing in freedom, then out of that joy it should also be possible to bring about changes of unjust and oppressive social and political conditions. We must only see beyond the moral necessity of repentance and learn to rejoice in it. The rule of law spoils everything, even the revolution of freedom.

4. The human play of liberated mankind

How does man become human? This is the question of men who have lost their humanity or have not yet found it. Here we shall discuss two men who did not know each other, Martin Luther and Karl Marx, and their respective ways, Reformation Christianity and revolutionary humanism.

Man makes himself human. Man is what he makes of himself, says the Aristotelian doctrine of virtue. 'Practice makes a master.' By doing justice over and over again, we become just men. By practising humanity we become true men. According to this conception, which at first glance is quite persuasive, man's humanity or inhumanity is up to man. He is always his own possibility. He can realize himself. He can also forfeit himself. But he remains the subject of his possibilities, even if in reality it often happens to be otherwise. But, in view of his actual inhumanity, is man really free? Does he not lose his ability to be human by the fact of his inhumanity? Does not his reality determine the opportunities remaining open to him? Does he not lose his freedom when he engages in unfreedom? How can an inhuman brute be transformed into a true human?

The liberation of man

The Christian belief in the gospel of God, which overcomes the law, has destroyed the naïve Aristotelian doctrine of virtue that at first seemed self-evident.[1] If man is what he makes of himself, then his *being human* depends on what he *does*. But what he does is subject to the law. The law, in turn, demands of him a justice he can no longer produce once he has become unjust. So he becomes the slave of a law which holds up to him a humanity it refuses to grant and demands of him freedom without setting him free. So, if man is what he makes of himself, he is precisely not free when it comes to his own actions but dependent on them and subject to them. Basically, they are the ones which make him, not he them. Luther called it blasphemy 'that our works create us or we are the creatures of our works. . . . We are our own gods, creators and producers.'[2] For him the basic principle of the Aristotelian doctrine of virtue becomes blasphemy when it is applied to the fundamental relationship of man to the ground of his existence, his relationship to God. He therefore rejected the anthropology of the self-made man and opposed it with the Christian anthropology expressed in the brief formula: 'Man is justified by faith' (*Hominem justificari fide*).[3] By this he meant that no form of action leads us from an inhuman to a human reality of man, for there is no way to get from doing to being.

What man is in his ground precedes what he does and manifests itself in his actions. His deeds do not change him fundamentally. Fundamental change occurs only by God's creative action upon him. When justification happens to a sinner, unjust living is made just. Only the gift of love turns an unloved being into a loved one. Like the *creation*, which happened without presuppositions, conditions, or requirements – *ex nihilo* or *de libertate dei*, as theological tradition used to put it – so the justification of the godless is the creative call of God to a new mode of being. 'Man is born anew,' says the language of the Bible. He is reborn by the world of love. Faith therefore is not a virtue, which can be learned, but more like a process of birth. God's trust *engenders* trusting faith in men. Theological language here abandons the realm of human productivity and draws its analogies from the generative sphere to distinguish doing from being.

That the new being of man is *engendered* by the calling, justifying and trusting word of Christ indicates a reversal of the relation between doing and being. 'We do not become just by doing justice, but because we have been justified, we do what is just,' says Luther against Aristotle. So works do not make the person, but a person does works. And the person is made by God. A person receives himself from God. The beloved therefore has died to the world of law and works and to the world of sin and death too. In death there are no prerogatives; of a dead man nothing can be demanded. Yet he lives in the new world of God 'where there is no law, no sin, no conscience, no death but utter joy, justice, peace, life, blessing and glory'.[4] And he acts out of that realm of freedom as long as he exists in this world of death. This means that man has been liberated from the coercive power of works (*necessitatis operum*). Man does not have to make himself. Rather he demonstrates his new being out of God by doing free works. He is no longer the unhappily proud creator-god of himself. He is no longer the creature of his works. He transcends all his works and stands facing them freely. Like God himself he steps back into hiding behind his works. His activities and the outward manifestations of his life no longer constitute 'his works' in the sense that he must constantly point to them and say, 'This I have done,' to have them serve as a monument to himself. He no longer has to identify with them to the extent that they become his idol. He has been freed from the care of monuments to himself.

Free works

The experience of being justified and loved by God establishes not only the freedom of a person in reference to his works but also 'free works'. Where man has been accepted and loved by God 'for nothing', his works become like Adam's in the garden: 'Which were altogether free works, done for the sake of nothing but to please God only and not to attain piety,' Luther wrote in the tract on *The Freedom of a Christian Man*.[5] Free works then are works freed from the purpose and the necessity to justify oneself. Like grace itself they too occur 'for nothing', that is, for the sake of pleasing God and out of love for the neighbour. Freed from self-assertion and self-searching, free works are done spontaneously, unselfishly, as if playing. They need not be compelled. They are taken for granted. The ethic of faith is love taken for granted and given freely without inner compulsion.

What Christian theology designates as *sanctification* following justification, as the *new obedience* in faith, as *Christian life* or *piety*, must then be described as categories radically different from those which denote man's bondage to the laws of achievement with their compulsions to act. The so-called *new obedience* is *new* only when it is no longer obedience but free, imaginative and loving action. The so-called *new law* is *new* only when it is no longer a law but the play of love which does the right whenever it does as it will. This does not mean that faith now comes under the *dominion of Christ* just as it had previously been dominated by the law, but it means that liberated faith freely enters the brotherhood of Christ.

In Romans 6, Paul developed the unfortunate parallel between the bondage of sin and the bondage of righteousness – and thus from one obedience to another – only 'because of your natural limitations', as he says in verse 19. He himself was evidently well aware of the weakness of his comparison. The freedom grasped by faith cannot be just a matter of 'exchanging dominions' in which one master is substituted for another and the structure of bondage is essentially left untouched. If in this freedom we are dealing with a 'happy change' (Luther), it has to be more like replacing the dictatorship of the law with the democracy of the spirit. The constitution of liberty bears no similarity at all to the constitution of bondage. New wine only spoils in old wineskins. When the liberated call Jesus 'lord', then that *lordship* is not what it once had been and otherwise is, for this lord is the crucified who has become the servant of all. He washes the tired feet of his own but he does not wash their heads ethically or their brains ideologically. The redeemer's power over the redeemed is derived from his sufferings. As their liberator he is the author of their liberty and thus their authority. Therefore their obedience is not blind, but it is free gratitude and the conscious practice of their freedom in creative love. This constitutes the free works.

Free relationships

'We wouldn't be so rough, if things were not so tough', states the *Threepenny Opera*. The person makes his works. That constitutes his freedom. In the biblical image, a good tree brings forth good fruit. The tree does not have to be forced to do this. It does it all by itself to display its riches and out of sheer joy of existence. But where do we find such a tree?

> The crippled tree in the yard
> Points to the bad soil.
> But the passers-by call it a cripple
> – and are right,

wrote Bert Brecht. Shall we then blame the bad fruit on bad soil as well as on bad roots? In a lightless yard a tree cannot be expected to blossom. It has no chance because of its environment which cripples the tree. But a tree planted in a park grows and develops fully.

'The noble origin of divine birth is the seal of the children of God; pride in accomplishments is the sign of bondage,' Hans Joachim Iwand has said beautifully.[6] But does not the modern achievement-centred society force men into that very bondage? In *Wilhelm Meister* Goethe recognized the end of a society based on representative nobility and the beginning of the age of the bourgeoisie. Consequently he advised citizens not to ask *Who are you?* but *What can you do?*[7] He clearly noted the transition from a society of class to an egalitarian society of achievements, from aristocracy to meritocracy. The latter is a society in which the categories of having and doing obscure the category of being, as the 'red rabbi' Moses Hess has argued. It measures man's social value solely by what he is able to produce, by his labour power, and by what he can afford to consume. Man derives his self-esteem and identity from what he has and what he can afford to have. He is aware of himself as a thing and experiences himself in the body he has, in money, house, children, social position, in the power and problems that are his. Instead of saying, 'I cannot sleep,' he says, 'I don't have the right sleeping pills.' Instead of saying, 'I love my wife,' he says, 'I have a happy marriage.' So man is not an existing self but translates everything into categories of having or not having. Apart from what he does or does not have he is nothing, does not exist and is not known.

Man is what he produces. He is what he makes of himself. With this Aristotelian principle Karl Marx criticized the capitalistic society of haves and have-nots. If this principle may be applied in anthropology, the wage earner in capitalistic societies is indeed exploited and alienated and thus deprived of his humanity. He produces profit for others. At the same time he produces his own poverty and inhumanity. Applying this same principle, Marx therefore demanded a *humane society* which produces men capable of enjoying the fullness and variety of their senses as a matter of course and enables men to produce themselves to the fullness of their own abilities. If we could translate Marx's critique of the capitalistic society of acquisitiveness back into the language of Luther, we would have to say: The exploiting *society of achievement* is a form of institutionalized justification by works. Its objective compulsion to worship the idols of its own achievements is nothing but organized blasphemy. Justification by works as practised by the mediaeval ecclesiastical society was child's play in comparison.

How can the crippled tree bring forth good fruit in these surroundings? How can man live a human life under such inhuman coercion?

Changing of self and the changing of conditions

In an achievement-centred society any attempt to liberate by faith man's inner *person* from the outward coercion of *works* leads only to a romantic escapade into the innermost recesses of the heart, unless it is accompanied by a *humanization of the structures* and principles of that society. The *liberation of persons* by faith must go hand in hand with free and *liberating works* of love, as Luther has said. When conditions are crippling the tree, these conditions must be changed so that the tree has an objective opportunity to develop freely. When social conditions force men to act in an inhuman way, these social conditions must be changed to give men an opportunity to act humanely. It is, of course, an illusion to believe that a prospective just society will automatically make all its members just and that a prospective free society will liberate all its members. Even the contention that unfree conditions necessarily produce slavish men is false. There always have been and still are men in bondage who have demonstrated and are demonstrating an amazing amount of independence and freedom. Otherwise, no social or political tyranny would ever have been overthrown. Conversely, external liberties do not guarantee the inner freedom of men. Under relatively free and just conditions there are a sufficiently large number of unfree and unjust men who fail to grasp the objective opportunities open to them. An unfree society does not automatically produce unfree men, but it does put men under such pressures that freedom becomes increasingly difficult for them. A relatively free society does not automatically produce free men, but it encourages their freedom.

Whether men actually avail themselves of the positive opportunities of being human depends less on conditions than on themselves. But we probably cannot discuss the *pressures of unfreedom* and the *encouragement* of freedom on wholly equal terms. Where the pressures of tyranny have become too great, the negative factors often have become stronger than men's personal strength to resist them. The encouragement derived from the positive factors in freedom does not work in the same way. It permits the exercise of freedom but does not preclude unfreedom. It does not prevent the abuse of freedom. So we may say with Aeschylus, 'Man loses half his virtue in bondage', but we may not deduce the converse, 'Man has already gained half of his virtue by freedom'. The many causes of human misfortune may be lessened. The pressures of bondage may be reduced. But this does not imply a guarantee of happiness and freedom. When this happens, and only then, it still depends on man to make the best of his opportunities. Inner and outward liberation belong together. One cannot be derived from the other. Marx therefore was right when in his famous third thesis he held against Feuerbach and materialism that the changing of self and of conditions are bound together in revolutionary, i.e., liberating, practice.[8]

The changing of self and of human personality without changing conditions is an *idealistic illusion* which theologians too should abandon.

The changing of conditions without changing man, on the other hand, is a *materialistic illusion* which the Marxists also should gradually leave behind.

The liberation of persons from the law of coercive achievement and the mitigation of objectivized necessities and built-in principles in our society are dialectically related. The freedom of a person, relieved by faith from the necessity of good works, and the hope for a liberated society, practised by loving the neighbour in bondage, are not contradictory principles but converge in actual living. To state it again theologically: *Following the crucified* liberates men from the laws and powers of this world and sets them free. The *iconoclasm of liberty* directed against the images, taboos and idols of society changes its conditions.

Can labour become creative play?

In the Marxist vision of the all-humane, i.e., Communist society, labour ceases to exist and is replaced by *self-induced activity*. Humanized man no longer works but lives his life in varied and meaningful activity. Exploitation is overcome through the socialization of the means of production. The division of labour and the confinement of men to particular and repetitive tasks will cease and will be replaced by well-rounded activities in the manner of artistic creativity. The future of the Marxist revolution is also a *vita aesthetica*, an aesthetic life. When Marx described the realm of liberty at all – and he did this remarkably seldom – he used aesthetic categories of playing, of the artist and of activities representing free people at their leisure. Marx constructed his vision of a future of *whole human beings* and the *free association of free individuals* out of Schiller's escapism into the realm of dreams where alone freedom blossoms. For the Czech Marxist Vítêzlav Gardavský *love* therefore becomes a key term 'which permits labour to turn into creativity and creativity into the means of human self-realization'. He feels that the deepest realization of man's humanity occurs in power-free, sincerely creative play and sees in this also a point of contact between Marxism and Christianity.[9] The French Marxist Roger Garaudy makes some helpful allusions along the same line: 'This kind of activity is going to have the marks of aesthetic activity.... Why should man be able to work only when he is spurred on by need and fear, particularly when the Christians themselves have invented a God whose creation is not a necessary emanation but an undeserved gift of love?'[10]

The old Marx was of course more cautious. 'Labour cannot become a form of play, as Fourier would like to have it', he says in *Das Kapital*. But the scope of leisure can be enlarged by automation in the sphere of necessary labour so that the actual humanization of man may eventually take place during leisure and need no longer be confined to labour. 'Labour always remains a realm of necessity. The development of human strength which is its own purpose, the true realm of freedom, always lies beyond it.'[11]

Since Marx we have become considerably more resigned at this point, because the history of industrialization – even of socialist industrialization – has shown that an increase in leisure time does not automatically assure an increase in human freedom or better opportunities for self-realization. That is why Herbert Marcuse and many of his fellow neo-Marxists have again taken up the ideas of Fourier. Marcuse contends in opposition to Marx: 'I believe that one of the new possibilities of demonstrating the qualitative difference between a free and an unfree society lies precisely in our ability to discover the realm of freedom *in* labour and not merely *beyond* it.'[12] If the separation of the realm of freedom from the realm of necessity is going to continue – as the old Marx felt constrained to insist – then men will have to live separate lives in each of these respective spheres. But that contradicts Marx's vision of the 'whole man'.

Marcuse insists that the modern development of the forces of production in highly industrialized societies affords an opportunity to realize freedom even *within* the realm of necessity and to transform the work day itself in such a way that its unnerving and stupefying aspects can be abolished and the process of production can become a creative process. Marcuse calls this *advance from Marx to Fourier* a movement 'from realism to surrealism'. To describe it he develops a utopia with aesthetic-erotic categories. The growing automation of the labour process demands of the worker a corresponding increase in self-reliance, productive imagination, and willingness to experiment. He becomes more of a 'guardian and regulator' of labour than its servant. Automation causes him to become the subject of freedom in the very realm of necessity. Whatever this may mean, the resolution of the conflict between necessity and freedom by the old Marx in terms of a quantitative progression of 'less work, more freedom' ultimately obscures the 'scandal of the qualitative difference' between an unfree and a free society, as Marcuse has said in another strange allusion to the Christian view.[13] What is the nature of this scandal, which even Marx ultimately evaded?

Anthropologically Marx continued to be tied to the *Aristotelian* doctrine of virtue according to which man is what he makes of himself – a creator of himself, a *causa sui*. The realm of freedom therefore can be built only on the foundations of the realm of necessity. Man is essentially a producer. If this is granted, man only has to produce humane conditions to become truly human. But this kept Marx closely tied to the capitalistic society of producers and held him firmly to its basic principle. He failed ideologically to break the 'compulsion of works' (*necessitas operum*) and confined himself to a reordering of that compulsion so that labour for the sake of others is changed into activity for its own sake and outside determination is replaced with self-determination. But if with the bourgeois enlightenment we move from *heteronomy* to *autonomy*, we must take care lest the *nomos* remain the same. It makes little difference whether we are subjected to an outside law or whether we make that law our own so that it appears to be our own law. The results are about the same. Whether we are chased by others or begin chasing ourselves, we still are the same chased animals. Autonomy also may be under the law. The achievement of self-determination itself may turn into pressure to achieve. Can we really use this legalistic structure to express the scandal of the qualitative difference between freedom and unfreedom? When we understand the change from *labour* to *creativity* in this way, creative playing still remains a tremendous achievement aimed at driving men to uncover their true humanity which still lies hidden in darkness.

The *Reformation alternative between justification by works and justification by faith* was considerably more radical. It was aware of the 'scandal of qualitative difference' between the works of the law, which brought Jesus to the cross, and the righteousness of the crucified, which justifies by faith 'without the works of the law'. When we apply this Reformation concept of man's justification by faith to the modern achievement-centred society, it implies that man is being liberated not only from outside determination and exploitation but in a much deeper sense also from the compulsive notion that he is what he produces. So he is not just set free from bad conditions of production merely to find himself in better ones. He need no longer be ashamed of himself and consequently he does not have to prove himself to himself any more. He finds his humanity in the awareness that he has already been accepted and loved as he is. This liberates him from alien laws and from himself, it does so in the sense that he no longer – in the dual meaning of the phrase – has to 'take his life' but may live and give it freely.

The religion of freedom

Can 'religion' help man to attain this freedom from himself? Feuerbach, with his capitalistic logic of producers, saw in religious images and feelings mere products of the human heart. Marx considered religion as the 'groaning of the creature in bondage' justified only by actual need and alienation. The revolution, therefore, was to become the heir of religion and would abolish the religious notions of wish-fulfilment by meeting actual needs and fulfilling concrete desires. But the historians of religion and culture Huizinga and van der Leeuw have shown that religion does not at all and in every instance originate in human *need* but is actually more likely an outcome of *play*, *representation* and *imagination*. In their festivals with the gods men did not only magically implore the gods' help in need, they also represented themselves and their lives before the totally-other, the gods, in order to regain a state of conformity with them as at the dawn of time.

The religion of ancient man, with its cults and festivals, was a form of playing. Ancient man demonstrated himself in covenant with the gods. He looked at history as a *feast of the gods*. Yet he suffered far greater material need than modern man. If this is granted, it follows that religion does not belong merely to the realm of necessity as the groaning of the creature in bondage – to use the language of Marx – but it also and more properly belongs to the realm of freedom as the play of remembrance, as an expression of joy, and as the imaginative hope of man's basic and final humanity before God. Religious myths and images are not just ideological tranquillizers which compensate for unbearable conditions or mitigate suppressed misery. They are daydreams of human communities in which the totally-other is made manifest, no matter how inappropriately, and where consequently the transformation of the here and now is already being anticipated. These communities are already celebrating that creative play which heavy-laden and labouring mankind longingly desires when it desires liberty. The 'religious Communist' Wilhelm Weitling was right after all, when in his *Gospel of the Poor Sinner* of 1843 he wrote: 'Religion must not be destroyed but used to liberate mankind. Christianity is the religion of liberty.'[14]

5. The liberating church – a testing ground of the kingdom of God

What is the purpose of the church? Many people today are asking this question. For some the question is a matter of *leavetaking*. They have been raised in a Christian environment, have enjoyed or rather endured confirmation instruction, have been baptized and married in the church, pay their church dues regularly, yet rarely take part in the 'life of the congregation', as they say in circles within the church. They identify with the church only sporadically, for example when they happen to enjoy a Christmas service or a special church rally (*Kirchentag*). Like all large organizations the established churches, the territorial and folk churches, suffer from a growing apathy of their members. This apathy no longer manifests itself primarily as partial identification with the church but increasingly as complete non-identification. Many functions in the lives of men, which the church used to exercise, have now been taken over by men themselves or by other cultural and social institutions. When a person has come to believe that the church has no function, he begins to question its customary presence at his domicile and in the schedule of his life. What is the purpose of the church? Shall he continue to support it in spite of the fact that it has little to say or to give to him?

For some people this becomes a *question of dread*. They identify fully with the church, and in view of its growing meaninglessness they get caught in an inner crisis of identity. Those who are experiencing this crisis tend to divide into two groups:

The one group would like to see the church become more *modern*, *involved*, *contemporary* and *relevant*. Since politics determine man's destiny, they are demanding the church's radical political involvement in the vital contemporary problems confronting their country and divided mankind. They look at the church as a political *avant-garde* on the road to justice and freedom in a world of conflicting interests and struggles for power. For them the ideal church is a moral vanguard of a better world.

The other group maintains that a church which is socially oriented, politically up to date and relevant is bound to lose its proper identity, its Christian *proprium*. They are at a loss to recognize the *church of their fathers* in a church which, for example, considers itself a sociotherapeutic institution. They too are aware that the number of those who still hold to the church is steadily declining. But they do not blame themselves or the church; rather they panic and extol their small number as the remnant of God's faithful during the final apostasy of mankind at the end of time. They retreat inwards into themselves and other like-minded circles where they can support each other. They make a virtue out of their necessity and change the *church* into a *sect*. Compared with active conformity to the modern world this is nothing but passive conformity. In confrontation with the 'flood of unbelief', which they bemoan, their own faith shrinks into little faith. They have lost confidence in him whom they believe. They fight for *pope and church* or *Bible and confession*. They want no 'experiments', no new experiences, and no dialogue with non-Christians. They are most adamant in their hostility toward those who share with them the experience of threatened identity and have chosen to act otherwise. So they contribute to the self-laceration of the church. The ghetto mentality continues to grow. Under the impact of the self-imposed retreat of the orthodox and the self-chosen challenges of the assimilators the self-confidence of the church is falling apart. The question of the church's purpose elicits a confusing variety of answers depending on the respective needs, but there is no longer a single, clear, and necessary answer.

In former times the church used to be regarded as the *crown of society*. State and social classes existed for the sake of the church, and the church existed for the sake of God and his necessary worship on earth. But then the state and the classes moved away from their religiously conceived end of worshipping God and – with Machiavelli – began to take religion and the churches into their service. 'The heads of a free state or an empire must uphold the supporting pillars of religion.' They will then find it easier 'to maintain their state religiously, hence beneficially and in unity . . . for religion greatly contributes to keeping the army obedient, the nation unified and the people virtuous', Machiavelli counselled in his famous *Prince* which was widely read by rulers and politicians.[1] According to Rousseau, each state needs a 'citizen's religion' to provide an ideal and symbolic bond of unity for its people. Here religion is no longer regarded in terms of *its own goals*, but it is judged and valued only on the basis of *its usefulness* for some other purpose. Religion may be used to maintain respect for the authority of princes, judges, teachers and fathers. Religion may be used to confront conflicting groups and parties with a higher point of view to establish harmony. Religion is necessary to support order, custom and morality in society. 'Let us preserve religion for the peoples! Thus religion ceases to be an end in itself and becomes a means to an end; its ends are determined by morality and politics.

When religion, church and faith are considered only from the standpoint of their expediency and usefulness for society, they are bound to vanish as soon as the purposes of society can be served by other means. 'The Moor has done his duty, the Moor may go' is then going to be the motto. Faith in God is no longer necessary to explain the riddles of nature or the turmoil of history. Nature and history can be explained *etsi Deus non daretur*, as if there were no God. Faith in God is no longer necessary to lead a decent life. Morality and ethical responsibility are an outcome of group behaviour. The church is no longer necessary to maintain authority in the various areas of living. Either the responsibilities have been democratized or the authorities maintain themselves without the support of religion.

Bourgeois society has emancipated itself from the guardianship of the church. Its members demand that they be considered of age in the use of their minds and wills. The movement toward emancipation in our society and the desire of each of its members for self-determination make it increasingly difficult to answer such questions as Why do we need the church? and What good does faith do? That is why some people are bemoaning the development toward emancipation as apostasy and others are frantically looking for human needs and problems still unsolved which may be used to demonstrate that the church and its faith are necessary after all.

Religion is meaningful in itself

The *crisis of identity* within the Christian community is not just a contemporary phenomenon. It has been discussed since the beginning of the European Enlightenment. We shall recall some of the ideas from that earlier discussion expressed by Schleiermacher in 1799, when in his work *On Religion* he addressed 'the cultured among its despisers'.[2] It was Schleiermacher's basic assumption that religion understood as a means to some other end already constitutes a falsification and misuse of religion. He had no intention to bring the educated of his time closer to religion with those kind of arguments. 'Do not be concerned that in the end I will still take my refuge in that common cure-all of telling you how necessary religion is to maintain justice and order in the world and to assist shortsighted human authority and limited human strength with a reminder of an all-seeing eye and of an infinite power; or that I will tell you what a wonderful friend and salutory support morality has in religion.' It would certainly be 'a wonderful thing, if heavenly religion could be expected to take reasonably good care of man's earthly affairs. . . . But for something like this it is hardly about to climb down from heaven.'

If religion does not constitute *its own end* and has no meaning or value in itself, then it has *no purpose* and meaning at all. Religion refuses to answer questions concerning its practical social value and its moral usefulness. Its dignity lies precisely in that it compels us to abandon this greedy and selfish line of questioning if we are to understand religion and have a part in it. Those who try to defend religion by establishing its external usefulness and necessity turn out to be its worst enemies in the long run. 'Whatever is loved and esteemed on the grounds of some external advantage may well be necessary, but it is not necessary for its own sake. Thus it may ever remain a pious desire which never becomes existing reality. No reasonable man is going to regard such a thing as having extreme value, but he will only pay a price in proportion to what he receives. For religion that price would be quite low. At least I, for one, would put in a very low bid. For I must confess, I do not believe that there is much merit in the contention that religion prevents unjust actions and brings about moral ones,' Schleiermacher maintained.[3] Religion therefore cannot be absorbed by the general circulatory processes of utilization in our modern society. If we try to fit it in any way, it will dissolve itself and be destroyed.

If the modern spheres of state, economy, education and morality have freed themselves from the influence of religion, God, faith and church – as it has often been shown – and if they now function by and in themselves, then this means negatively an end of the dominant position of religion in society, but it also means positively that religion, God, faith and the church have finally been liberated from their role as helpers in need and may now be themselves again. There is no need to panic when old necessities for religion are falling apart. We ought to think of the positive opportunities arising in this new situation. In my view, these lie in the Augustinian reversal of the relationship between religion and life.

The Augustinian reversal

After men have been *using* God for such a long time to enjoy the world, or at least to survive in it, God certainly does not promptly have to disappear from a world in which he is no longer needed for that purpose. If faith will only reflect on its true nature, we may come to a reversal of the things we enjoy and the things we use. Then man will *use the world to enjoy God*. The God who is a helper in need may disappear slowly but surely from the lives of many people and from our society as a whole. After the 'death' of this God we are going to be able to talk about the free God and how we can 'enjoy' him.[4] When we cease using God as *helper in need*, *stop-gap* and *problem solver*, we are – according to Augustine – finally free for the *fruitio Die et se invicem in Deo*, the joy of God and the enjoyment of each other in God. Purpose-free rejoicing in God may then take the place of the uses and abuses of God.

When theology is no longer necessary to practise philanthropy, it certainly will not have to disappear, but it may then finally be done for God's own sake and out of infinite rejoicing in God, which is in keeping with its true nature. As the church is being discharged from the social functions it has served until now, it does indeed become superfluous in these areas. In a world characterized by an eternal return of the same purposes and utilization processes the only really interesting thing may well turn out to be what is superfluous. In an industrialized, then highly industrialized, and finally – with Herman Kahn – post-industrial society it would seem that economy and industry will become increasingly less interesting. Who could possibly be passionately involved in processes which are automated or cybernetically controlled?

The First Liberated Men in Creation

Growing industrialization will give men greater freedom from the pressures of mechanical and degrading forms of labour. But when men are working for increasingly shorter periods of time, the problem is going to arise: Who may still be working? This will make it impossible to maintain the basic thesis on which our image of man, our whole educational and ethical system had been built until now, namely that man is justified and made respectable by his work. Man will have considerably more freedom from work than before. But he will be free for what, and how is he going to experience his freedom? Will his freedom make him feel the dread of his own redundancy? Will his work vanish without a trace, without leaving any imprint of his personal presence in life? Is life, in which labour is losing its meaning, going to be empty? Will man consider himself irrelevant because he is no longer needed as he once was? Or is he finally going to use his automated world of labour to enjoy God's beauty and the value of his own existence? The man who has been raised by the motto that work alone makes life enjoyable is going to be in for a very rough time. A man who values himself in terms of his usefulness to society must consider his life useless when he is no longer needed. Those who equate the meaning of life with having purposes are bound to experience the lack of purpose as meaninglessness.

Schleiermacher presented religion as *meaningful in itself* but externally *not necessary*. He combined the concept of the intrinsic value of religion with social criticism of enslaving labour. 'Millions of people of either sex and all social classes are now moaning under the burdens of mechanical and degrading labour. . . . There is no greater impediment to religion than that we must be our own slaves; for everyone who must work at tasks which properly should be done by brute strength is a slave. We hope that the perfection of the arts and sciences will make this brute strength serviceable to us so that the physical world and the governable part of the mental world may be changed into a fairy-tale palace. . . . Only then will every man be freeborn, then every life will be practical and contemplative at once, the rod of the slave-driver will then be lifted against no one and every man will have rest and leisure to reflect on the world in himself.'[5]

We still are a long way from this kind of Augustinian reversal of the *use of God* and the *enjoyment of God*. Whether sciences and technologies ever will change the world into a fairy-tale palace is rather doubtful in view of the destruction of nature by modern technology. It is also basically unnecessary to speculate about freedom and religion in a post-industrial society in order to discuss the Augustinian reversal. Whatever the external conditions may be, reversal belongs to the core of the Christian faith as such. If the Christian faith is fundamentally liberation from the works of the law into the liberty of the children of God, then faith itself must constantly press for practical steps which lead men from the realm of necessity into the realm of freedom. Rejoicing in the free God and in its own liberty, faith must and will advance beyond the legal and completely capitalistic question: What is the use of God and for what is faith useful? We do not believe freely because it helps us spiritually. We do not pray freely if need has taught us to pray. We do not go to church because it may be to our advantage. We do not properly study theology because it may come in handy later on. We believe insofar as we confront the believable. We pray because it is the privilege of the liberated to talk with God. We go to church because it is a joy to do so when the service is enjoyable. We study theology properly because we are curious and find pleasure in the subject.

Experiments in the realm of freedom

Having lost its position as necessary support of the state and its class structure, the contemporary church finds itself increasingly confined to the *sphere of rendering service* to society. Our functionally organized society rarely thinks of the church from the external political viewpoint of 'throne and altar,' but it is apt to regard the church as helpful in specific areas of life. These areas – sociologically speaking – are the service sector. The church's care and concern is invited in matters of child raising, visiting the sick, the aged and the imprisoned, and in the field of personal morality. Its services are needed at certain critical or crucial moments in life such as birth, graduation, marriage, sickness, marital conflict and death. The common element in all these is that they concern areas of life which are relatively free from domination and are confined to times which are relatively free from labour. Here our present society – and perhaps even the best of possible societies – is revealing needs which may properly be called religious needs.

Contemporary criticism of the church, on the other hand, is exclusively directed against its so-called 'meddling' in politics, business and education whenever this is regarded as undesirable interference. Of course, these more recent areas of religious needs in the private spheres of human life do not render the church and its services less necessary than it formerly used to be in the spheres of public order and morality.

Here it must be clearly and critically stated that the modern *emancipatory society* makes freedom possible exclusively for those who are competent and healthy, who have already succeeded and are able to enjoy themselves.[6] Its humanistic ideals of man's coming of age and of man's autonomy have paradoxically contributed to a tendency which turns contemporary society into a *segregated society*. Children are sent to kindergartens, the aged to homes for senior citizens, the sick to hospitals, the incurable to nursing homes, criminal elements to prisons and reformatories, etc. The rest then are left alone and undisturbed. Today, due to our longer life expectancy, more generations are living at one time than in former societies, when a generation still counted as thirty years. Now it has stretched to sixty or seventy years. The longer generations are forced to live together the more they seek separation, the more it seems that the young and fit are crowding all others out of the centres of life. Who is going to speak up for the suppressed liberties of the displaced, for the freedom to grow old, the freedom to be a child, the freedom to be sick, the freedom to receive love and to experience community, the freedoms of the aged, the young, the suffering and the guilty? This 'OK world', which leaves nothing to be desired, is an illusion created for quite transparent reasons.

Even in the so-called emancipated society there remains sufficient need and misery urgently calling for the practice of the freedom of faith and love. And since our enlightened society produces a frightening amount of new suffering and new displacements, it is bound to be upset by the practice of the Christian freedom of love in its alleys and basements. If Christians and ecclesiastical institutions are really serious about practising the liberty of Christ which is the hope of the hopeless, they will have no trouble keeping busy in our society and are in no danger of unemployment.

At the same time we note an expansion of the realm characterized by the absence of primary desires and external needs. I am speaking of the *realm of leisure*, of relaxation, entertainment and culture, the realm of purpose-free sociability. Christian congregations really do not know what to do with this area. So they fill it with theological workshops and charitable or social activities. In view of the make-up of contemporary society this is not necessarily objectionable. But Schleiermacher looked at this area relatively free of domination and labour in another way. In his *Theory of Social Behaviour* (1802) he found that 'all cultured human beings – as one of their first and most noble desires – are seeking free fellowship bound and determined by no external purpose'. He already envisioned the goal of emancipation to be the free and unlimited communication between free men, as Jürgen Habermas now calls it. In such a purpose-free fellowship he saw the fulfilment of the goals of the French Revolution on the religious and artistic levels, namely *brotherhood* in the spirit of *liberty* on the ground of *equality*. He considered fellowship as the free play of the human spirit in conversation, in the arts, in productive imagination and in the rejoicing of men with each other. In this sphere he saw the realization of democracy, which had not been realized politically, since here the *reversing effect* of free give and take was already setting aside the strict order of rank in the political world of his time. But he admitted that this social democracy existed only within the free circles and salons of the educated and wealthy. He did hope, as we have seen, that the sciences would someday liberate man from the slavery of mechanical labour. But as things were, free fellowship was available only to the 'lucky few'. They could already anticipate in their own time the future realm of democracy where true religion flourishes. For the unfortunate, therefore, they represented the future for which it supposedly paid to work. Schleiermacher's vision did not lead to an aggressive critique of the world of labour. Still, there is something here which we ought not to discard.

If we now take another critical look at the *expanding scope of man's leisure*, we note first of all that this does not necessarily imply open space for free humanity at all. As a rule, the free play of relaxation and recreation offers no real alternatives to the world of labour. The determining factors in our relaxation and recreation are the very tensions which make them necessary. In our leisure we replay the very same things we have endured in our work and business, only without coercion and necessity. Workers at rattling machines relax on crackling motor-cycles, and professors, who read and write books, unwind with detective stories. In fact, most of our compensating and relaxing sociability reflects our work in society and occurs in conjunction with it. Why else are we talking so much about our business, university, household problems and the training of our children? We cannot *turn off* after all and are unable to make ourselves talk about something entirely different. Free sociability is not free but is governed by reproductive imagination, which we employ in an attempt to free ourselves from our problems by talking them over again. If it were otherwise, workers would read books and professors would ride motor-bikes and one would not immediately be able to guess the professions of people sitting around a table by the topics of their conversation.

The steps leading from a *reproduction of the working world* during leisure to the *production of new conditions in leisure* are difficult but must be attempted if we are to live our freedom actually. This is why Christian congregations should not use their allotted portion of the time free of labour and domination entirely for educational and socio-ethical activities. These activities may be necessary but they are not yet free. Christians should experiment with the possibilities of creative freedom. By this we do not mean the kinds of conversation, fellowship and games which only serve to provide necessary relaxation from the tensions caused by the excessive demands of everyday living. This also is important but it is not yet free. But it does mean that at these points we try to play out models of creative freedom. Following up on the *reproductive imagination* which updates the past, it means to encourage *productive imagination* which looks toward the future; and it means to bring back to light man's repressed *spontaneity*. It means to support a culture which does not merely offer social compensations but prepares for social change by introducing people to an unauthoritarian brotherhood. Worship itself may become a source of this new spontaneity; it no longer has to be a place of inhibitions, embarrassments and polite efforts. Christian congregations may then become testing grounds of the realm of freedom right in the realm of necessity. It is only natural to ask for examples and prescriptions of how this can be *done*. Examples and prescriptions can only inhibit spontaneity which, after all, cannot be *done* but only released or set free. I have actually seen the signs of the liberated church: at Ascension Church in East Harlem, at the 'liberated church' in San Francisco, in black congregations in Kenya, in German congregations abroad and Christian groups within the German church which definitely did not consist solely of young people. A person has to try this out for himself to experience it.[7]

Being-there-for-others is an important matter. Dietrich Bonhoeffer used this formula to illuminate the mystery of Christ's vicarious living and dying *for us*. Being-there-for-others also is the secret of love with those who follow the man from Nazareth. Being-there-for-others is the fundamental structure of Christ's church which vicariously speaks up for men and particularly represents those who have no one to speak for them. Being-there-for-others is essential for the liberation and redemption of human life that has been oppressed and become guilty. Love is the concrete expansion of liberty. These basic insights have led to the now generally accepted formulas of the *church-for-the-world* and the *church-for-others*. They, in turn, have developed into specific forms of action such as *Bread for the World* (World Service), *Amnesty for Prisoners*, *Christmas of Solidarity*, telephone ministries, etc. Love, suffering with others and speaking up for their happiness, is indeed the currently required form of freedom in the midst of bondage and forsakenness.

Still, being-there-for-others is not the final answer, nor is it an end and not even freedom itself. It is a way, although the only way, which leads to *being-there-with-others*. Christ's death *for us* has its end and future in that he is *with us* and that we shall be living, laughing and ruling *with him*. Being-there-for-others in vicarious love has as its end to be *with others* in liberty. Giving bread to the world's hungry has as its end to break our bread *with all mankind*. If this is not our end, our care for others merely becomes a new kind of domination. *Church for others* may easily lead us back to the old paternalism, unless its ultimate end is that kingdom where no one needs to speak up for the other any more but where each person rejoices with his neighbour and all men enjoy themselves together. *Being-there-for-others* is the way to the redemption of this life. *Being-there-with-others* is the form which the redeemed and liberated life itself has taken. The church therefore must not regard itself as just a means to an end, but it must demonstrate already in its present existence this free and re-

deemed being-with-others which it seeks to serve. In this sense –
and only in this sense – the church is already an end in itself, not as
church complete with hierarchy and bureaucracy but as the
congregation of the liberated. In that sense the church's function
reaches beyond rendering assistance to a troubled world; it does
already possess its own *demonstrative value of being*. In the remembered
and hoped-for liberty of Christ the church serves the liberation
of men by demonstrating human freedom in its own life and
by manifesting its *rejoicing in that freedom*.

Notes to 'The Liberation of "God"'

1. Preface, above, p. vi.
2. See above, p. 80.
3. Preface, above, p. vi.
4. See above, p. 39.
5. See above, p. 43.
6. See above, p. 58f.
7. See above, p. 59.
8. See above, p. 71ff.
9. See above, p. 49.
10. See above, p. 61f.
11. See above, p. 80.
12. The Westminster Press, Philadelphia 1972, esp. pp. 51–9.
13. Op. cit., p. 54.
14. Op. cit., p. 55.
15. Op. cit., pp. 56f.
16. Op. cit., pp. 57f.
17. Op. cit., p. 58.
18. Op. cit., p. 59.
19. See above, p. 62.
20. See above, p. 50.
21. See above, p. 63f.
22. Referred to at p. 19 above.
23. See above, p. 17.

Notes to 'The First Liberated Men in Creation'

Domination through games and the preparatory games of liberation

1. F. J. J. Buytendijk, *Hit spel van mensch en dier als openbaring van levendriften*, Amsterdam 1932; also 'Der Spieler', *Das Menschliche*, Stuttgart 1958, pp. 208–29; J. Huizinga, *Homo Ludens. Vom Ursprung der Kultur im Spiel*, Hamburg 1956; F. G. Jünger, *Die Spiele*, List Bücher 128, 1959; H. Rahner, *Der spielende Mensch*, Einsiedeln 1952; E. Fink, *Spiel als Weltsymbol*, Stuttgart 1960.
Of the more recent theological works we note the following: D. Sölle, *Phantasie und Gehorsam*, Stuttgart 1968; H. Buhr, *Das Glück und die Theologie*, Stuttgart 1969; G. M. Martin, *Wir wollen hier auf Erden schon . . .* , Stuttgart 1970; Harvey Cox, *The Feast of Fools. A Theological Essay on Festivity and Fantasy*, London 1969; D. L. Miller, *Gods and Games: Toward a Theology of Play*, New York 1970; R. E. Neale, *In Praise of Play: Toward a Psychology of Religion*, New York 1969; A. A. van Ruler, *Gestaltwerdung Christi in der Welt. Über das Verhältnis von Kirche und Kultur*, Neukirchen 1956; V. Gardavsky, *Hoffnung aus der Skepsis*, Munich 1970.
2. F. Schiller, *Über die ästhetische Erziehung des Menschen*, first ed. 1793, second ed. 1795.
3. N. S. Lesskow, 'Die Teufelsaustreibung', *Weg aus dem Dunkel*, Leipzig 1952, pp. 190–207.
4. Cf. H. M. Enzensberger, *Einzelheiten I, Bewusstseinsindustrie*, Frankfurt 1964.
5. G. Lukács, *Ästhetik, Teil I*, 2. Halbband, Neuwied 1963, pp. 577ff.; Lukács stresses the 'characteristic of suspension implicit in the aesthetic sphere'. In aesthetic activity man rests from the necessity of acting.
6. H. Cox, op. cit., p. 22.
7. G.W. F. Hegel, *Ästhetik*, Berlin 1955, p. 95.
8. M. McLuhan, 'Introduction to the second edition', *Understanding Media: The Extension of Man*, New York 1964.
9. K. Marti, *Leichenreden*, Neuwied 1969, pp. 62f.

The theological play of the good will of God

1. E. Fink, op. cit., p. 237.
2. This is the alternative posed by A. van Ruler toward the end of his work cited above, n. 1.
3. H. Rahner, op. cit., p. 15.
4. For a comparison of these two pronouncements, cf. D. L. Miller, 'The Kingdom of Play: Some Old Theological Light from Recent Literature', *Union Seminary Quarterly Review*, XXV, 1970, pp. 343–60.
5. Cf. also H. Gollwitzer, *Krummes Holz – aufrechter Gang*, Munich 1970, pp. 177ff.
6. F. J. J. Buytendijk, 'Der Spieler', *Das Menschliche*, Stuttgart 1958, p. 210.

The First Liberated Men in Creation

7. Cf. ibid., pp. 210f.
8. Cf. also H. F. Schultz, *Auch Gott ist nicht fertig*, Stuttgart 1969, pp. 133 f.
9. E. Bloch, *Zur Ontologie des Noch-Nicht-Seins*, Frankfurt 1961, pp. 15ff.
10. There is at this point an interesting parallel between William James and Ernest Bloch. At the occasion of the centennial of James' birth in 1942 Bloch gave a lecture at Cambridge, Mass., in which he quoted James as saying: 'Realities float in a huge ocean of possibilities from which they have to be selected' (Bloch, *Philosophische Aufsätze*, Frankfurt 1969, p. 64). His previously cited work *Zur Ontologie des Noch-Nicht-Seins* (1961, p. 32) contains the same image in similar language from his own pen: 'Existing reality is surrounded by an ocean of possibilities, and out of this ocean, again and again, new bits and pieces of reality still rise to the surface. . . .' The influence of the restless American soul from that land of (supposedly) unlimited opportunities on Bloch's philosophical imagery is therefore not so limited as some have assumed. Today, with its new interest in play, festivity, and meditation young America is trying to shake off its compulsion of doing things, which is implicit in the American faith in progress, and to 'cool down history'. Cf. Harvey Cox, op. cit., pp. 46ff.
11. In this distinction between *production* and *representation* I am referring to anthropological phenomena which have been investigated by H. Plessner. Cf. H. Plessner, 'Zur Anthropologie des Schauspielers', *Zwischen Philosophie und Gesellschaft*, Bern 1953, pp. 180–92.
12. Buytendijk, 'Der Spieler', p. 229.
13. Cf. also G. M. Martin, op. cit., pp. 79ff.
14. Harvey Cox, 'God and the Hippies', *Playboy* 1968, p. 15.
15. H. Rahner, op. cit., p. 52.
16. Harvey Cox, *The Feast of Fools*, pp. 139ff.
17. F. Flögel, *Geschichte des Groteskekomischen. Ein Beitrag zur Geschichte der Menschheit*, Leignitz/Leipzig 1788. This volume contains many examples of the *risus paschalis*, the Easter laughter.
18. W. Benjamin, *Ursprung des deutschen Trauerspiels*, Frankfurt 1963, p. 183.
19. M. Luther, WA, XXXVI, p. 600; XLV, p. 356.
20. Cf. F. Rosenzweig, *Der Stern der Erlösung*, Heidelberg 1954, pp. 176f. According to St Thomas also, eternity appears in time as enticing and desired future.
21. K. Barth, *Church Dogmatics* II, 1, pp. 650, 655.
22. Cf. the article 'doxa', TDNT II, pp. 240ff.
23. J. Schniewind, *Die Freude der Busse*, Göttingen 1956.

The human play of liberated mankind

1. For the following I am indebted to H. J. Iwand's Luther interpretation: 'Glaubensgerechtigkeit nach Luther's Lehre', *Th Ex heute* 75, Munich 1941.
2. WA, XXXIX, I, p. 48.
3. 'Disputatio de homine', WA, XXXIX, I, pp. 175ff. Cf. also E. Wolf, 'Menschwerdung des Menschen', *Peregrinato II*, 1965, pp. 119ff., especially 133f.
4. M. Luther, WA, XL, I, p. 45.
5. Luther, *De Libertate Christiana*, cap. 22.
6. H. Iwand, op. cit., p. 49.
7. J. Habermas, *Öffentlichkeit*, Neuwied 1962, p. 23.
8. 'The materialistic doctrine of changing the conditions and educational

processes is overlooking the fact that conditions must be changed by men and that the educator himself must be educated. It is therefore obliged to separate society into two parts one of which has to be superior to him. The concurrence of the changing of conditions and of the human activity of self-transformation can therefore be taken and rationally comprehended only in the form of *revolutionary practice.*' Karl Marx, *Frühschriften*, ed. Landshut, Stuttgart 1953, pp. 339f.

9. V. Gardavsky, op. cit., pp. 52ff.
10. R. Garaudý, *Der Dialog*, rororo aktuell 944, 1966, p. 86.
11. Marx, *Das Kapital*, III, Berlin 1959, pp. 873f.
12. H. Marcuse, *Versuche über die Befreiung*, Suhrkamp edition 329, 1969, pp. 40ff.; *Das Ende der Utopie*, Berlin 1967, 12f.
13. H. Marcuse, *Das Ende der Utopie*, p. 20.
14. W.Weitling, *Das Evangelium des armen Sünders*, Bern 1845, p. 17.

The liberating church — a testing ground of the kingdom of God

1. For a history of the origins of 'political religion' cf. J. Moltmann, 'Theologische Kritik der Politischen Religion', Moltmann, Metz, Oelmüller, *Kirche im Prozess der Aufklärung*, Munich/Mainz 1970, pp. 20ff.
2. Quoted from an edition in the philosophical library of Felix Meiner, Leipzig, no date, p. 23.
3. Ibid., p. 26.
4. W. Hamilton as quoted by S. Daecke, *Der Mythos vom Tode Gottes*, Stundenbücher 87, Hamburg 1969, pp. 48ff. Cf. also J. Moltmann, 'Zukunft als neues Paradigma der Transzendenz', *Internationale Dialog Zeitschrift*, vol. 2, 1969, 1, pp. 6f.
5. Schleiermacher, op. cit., p. 144.
6. J. B. Metz, 'Gefährliche und befreiende Erinnerung. Zur Präsenz der Kirche in der Gesellschaft', *Publik* 1970, 41, p. 23.
7. Cf. Sister Corita, *Footnotes and Headlines. A Play-Pray-Book*, New York 1967.